ILLUSTRAT
MICROSOFT
EXCEL

Paul Herzlich

David Fulton Publishers
London

David Fulton Publishers Ltd
2 Barbon Close
London WC1N 3JX

First published in Great Britain by
David Fulton Publishers 1991

British Library Cataloguing in Publication Data
Herzlich, Paul
    Illustrated Microsoft Excel.
    1. Microcomputer systems. Spreadsheet packages
    I. Title
    005.365

    ISBN 1-85346-152-0

Designed by Almac Ltd, London
Typeset by Chapterhouse, The Cloisters, Formby
Printed in Great Britain by
Martins of Berwick

Contents

Introduction

Microsoft Excel is a computer program used primarily to analyse and present numerical data. It is among the leaders in a class of personal computer software called spreadsheets which do for numbers what word processors do for text.

A spreadsheet is organised into columns and rows like an accountant's worksheet. But unlike a worksheet on paper, every position on a spreadsheet is capable of operating like an electronic programmable calculator. In Excel, you enter a combination of raw data and formulas on a spreadsheet and when you change your raw data, the results of the formulas are automatically recalculated and redisplayed instantly.

Making sense of numbers is often a matter of presentation so Excel provides a rich set of features for turning your data into clear charts with just a few mouse clicks or keystrokes. You can display graphs on screen for instant analysis of changes to your data and print out high quality charts to include in reports and presentations.

The tabular format of a spreadsheet is also ideally suited for storing a database. Excel has useful features for sorting and querying data which integrate seamlessly with the flexibility of the spreadsheet. In fact, all of Excel's features can be tied together by its macro programming language which enables you to write complete applications for invoicing, sales, stock and much more.

Excel for Microsoft Windows

This book is written for users of all versions of Excel under Microsoft's Windows Presentation Manager running under MS- and PC-DOS. Users of Excel in other environments will find the essentials of the program very similar or identical.

To use this book . . .

Sit at the keyboard and find the page which illustrates a task similar to your own. Follow the commands on the illustration and if you need more information refer to the instructions and tips on the facing page.

If you're new to spreadsheets or to Microsoft Windows, it's best to work through the examples at least once from the beginning of the book until you have mastered the basics. At the back of the book you'll find a reference section with details of Excel's keys, commands and functions.

Helpful tips

You'll see the 'Helpful tips' heading on nearly every instruction page in this book. The tips give shortcuts, advise on how to avoid pitfalls and explain alternatives to the illustrated techniques. Here's your first tip:

Excel has a very comprehensive 'Help' facility based on hypertext technology. To get help virtually anywhere in the program, press **F1**. The Help menu also includes Excel's Tutorial and Feature Guide which are interactive lessons on how to use Excel.

Starting

Before you can work with Excel, the program and the Microsoft Windows operating environment must be installed on your hard disk. Follow the instructions in the Excel manuals.

Starting Excel

- If you have a full copy of Windows version 3.0 or higher, Excel is installed as an application that can be started from the Program Manager. Select the Excel icon and press **Enter** or double-click on it with the mouse. If you have a full copy of Windows earlier than version 3.0 (including Windows/386), select EXCEL.EXE from the MS-DOS Executive.
- If you have Excel with a Run Time version of Windows. Excel runs from the DOS prompt like any other DOS application. Change to the subdirectory where the program is installed: for example, if you have used the standard installation options, type **CD\WINDOWS** and press **Enter**. Then type **EXCEL** and press **Enter**.

Windows basics

There is a regular pattern to working with a Windows application. First you *select* an object on the screen, then you *act* by typing in data or choosing a command from a menu. For example in Excel, first you select an area of a worksheet, then you enter data into the selected area. A selected object is highlighted as white lettering on a black background, or is surrounded by a dotted border. At any given moment, something is always selected.

Selecting and acting using the mouse

Move the mouse pointer over the object that you want to select, then *click*, which means to press and release the mouse button once. Use the left mouse button for all mouse operations, unless you have customised Windows to reverse the buttons. To select a large area, point to the beginning of the area, press the mouse button, *drag* the mouse pointer across to the end of the area, then release the mouse button. Cancel the selection by clicking on – selecting – something else. Some parts of the screen have built in actions which are triggered by a *double-click* which means press the mouse button twice in quick succession.

Selecting and acting using the keyboard

Press the arrow keys to move the selection. Press and hold the **Shift** key while using the arrow keys to select an area. Cancel the selection by moving the arrow keys which automatically selects something else. Once an object is selected, pressing **Enter** is the signal to act.

Helpful tips

Pointing and clicking with the mouse is simple but sometimes inefficient. Most of your work in Excel involves keying in data and formulas so in this book we assume you will mostly use the keyboard. If you have one of the more recent versions of Excel, you may see a Tool Bar at the top of the screen that provides shortcuts for performing many tasks with a mouse.

To leave Excel, press **Alt, F, X**. Excel will ask you whether you want to save any unsaved work. *Do not switch off the computer until you have saved your work*, a process which is illustrated in *Entering Data*.

3

Windows Commands

If you are already familiar with Windows, you may wish to skip this illustration.

Menus

You choose Excel commands from pull-down menus at the top of the screen.

Mouse procedure: Point to the menu name in the Menu Bar, press and hold the mouse button, drag to a command on the menu, and release the mouse button to choose it. Alternatively, click on the menu name in the menu bar, then click on the command on the menu. Drag or click the pointer off the menu to roll up the menu without selecting a command.

Keyboard procedure: Press the **Alt** key, press the letter underlined on the Menu Bar, then press the underlined letter of the command on the menu. Alternatively, press **Alt**, use the arrow keys to pull down the menu and select a command, and press **Enter** to execute the command. Press **Esc** to leave the menu without picking a command.

Commands shown on a menu in feint grey are unavailable in the current context of what you are doing. Items followed by three dots lead to a *Dialogue Box* where you enter further information.

Dialogue Boxes

A *Fill-in* on a dialogue box requires you to type in some text. Some Fill-ins are associated with a *List Box*. Selecting an item in the list automatically does the fill-in. A *Check Box* switches an option on and off. An 'X' appears in the Check Box when the option is switched on. A Check Box is grey when the option is 'on' in some parts of the area currently selected and 'off' in other parts. *Option Buttons* work like a TV remote control. Selecting one option automatically deselects the others. *Command Buttons* carry out an action. Most dialogue boxes have OK and Cancel command buttons. OK carries out the command. Cancel closes the box and cancels the command. The button with a thick outline is the default command for closing the box.

Mouse procedure: To move around a dialogue box, click on the item or button. Use a simple click to: select from a List Box; switch a Check Box on or off; select one of a group of Option Buttons; execute the command on a Command Button.

Keyboard procedure: Press **Tab** to move from item to item on the box. To go directly to an item, press *and hold down* **Alt**, then press the underline letter. Once an item is selected: use arrow keys to select a line in a List Box; press **Spacebar** to check or un-check a Check Box; press arrow keys to select an Option Button; press **Spacebar** to press a Command Button. **Esc** presses the Cancel button and **Enter** presses the command button with the thick outline (usually OK).

Helpful tips

Only press **Enter** after you have completed *all* your entries on the dialogue box. To leave a Fill-in and move to another item, use **Tab**, or **Alt** and an underlined letter, instead of **Enter**.

Key names appear in this book in **bold** type. Two key names separated by a comma, like **Alt, F**, means you press the first key then the second. A plus sign between two keys, like **Alt+T**, means you press and hold the first key, then press the second. For shortcuts that allow you to issue menu commands directly from the keyboard, refer to the *Excel Reference* at the back of this book.

Windows Commands

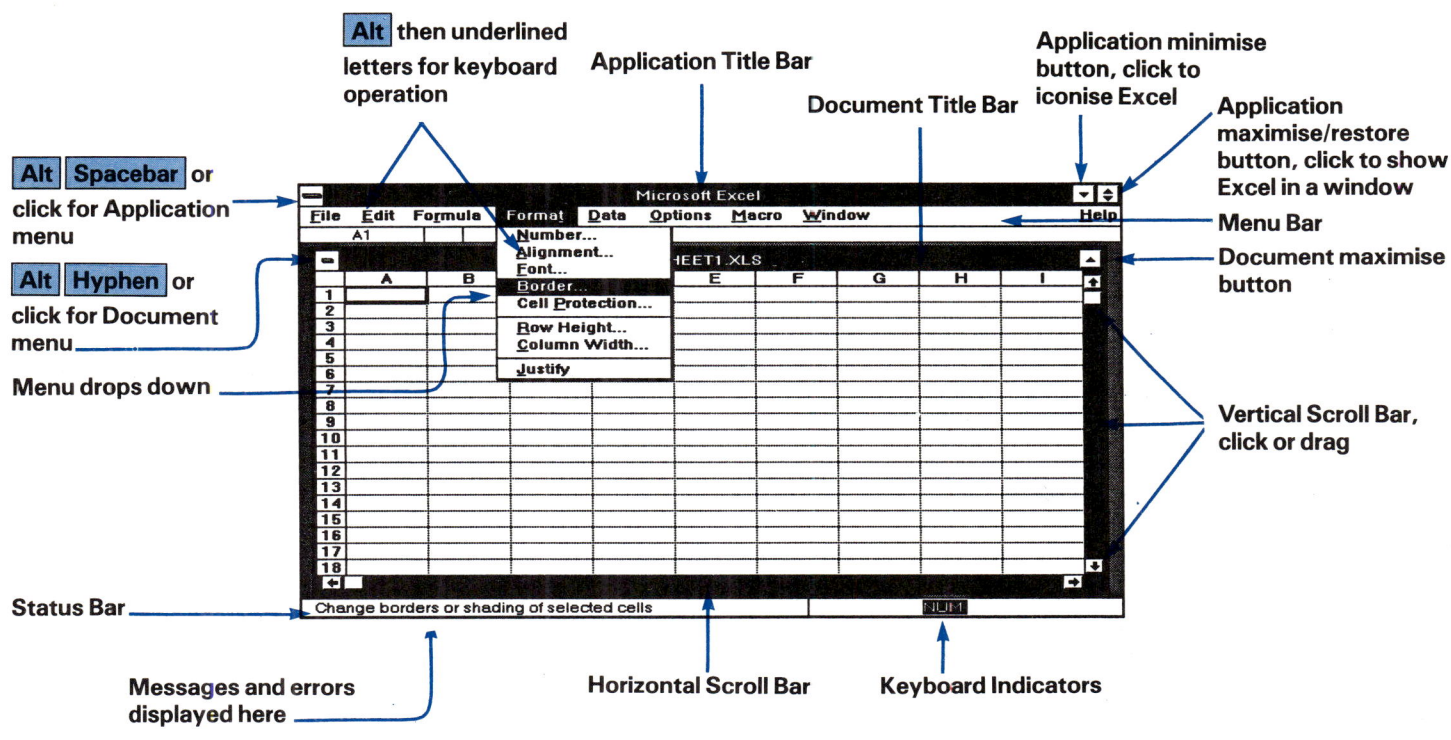

Alt then underlined letters for keyboard operation

Application Title Bar

Document Title Bar

Application minimise button, click to iconise Excel

Alt **Spacebar** or click for Application menu

Application maximise/restore button, click to show Excel in a window

Alt **Hyphen** or click for Document menu

Menu Bar

Document maximise button

Menu drops down

Vertical Scroll Bar, click or drag

Status Bar

Messages and errors displayed here

Horizontal Scroll Bar

Keyboard Indicators

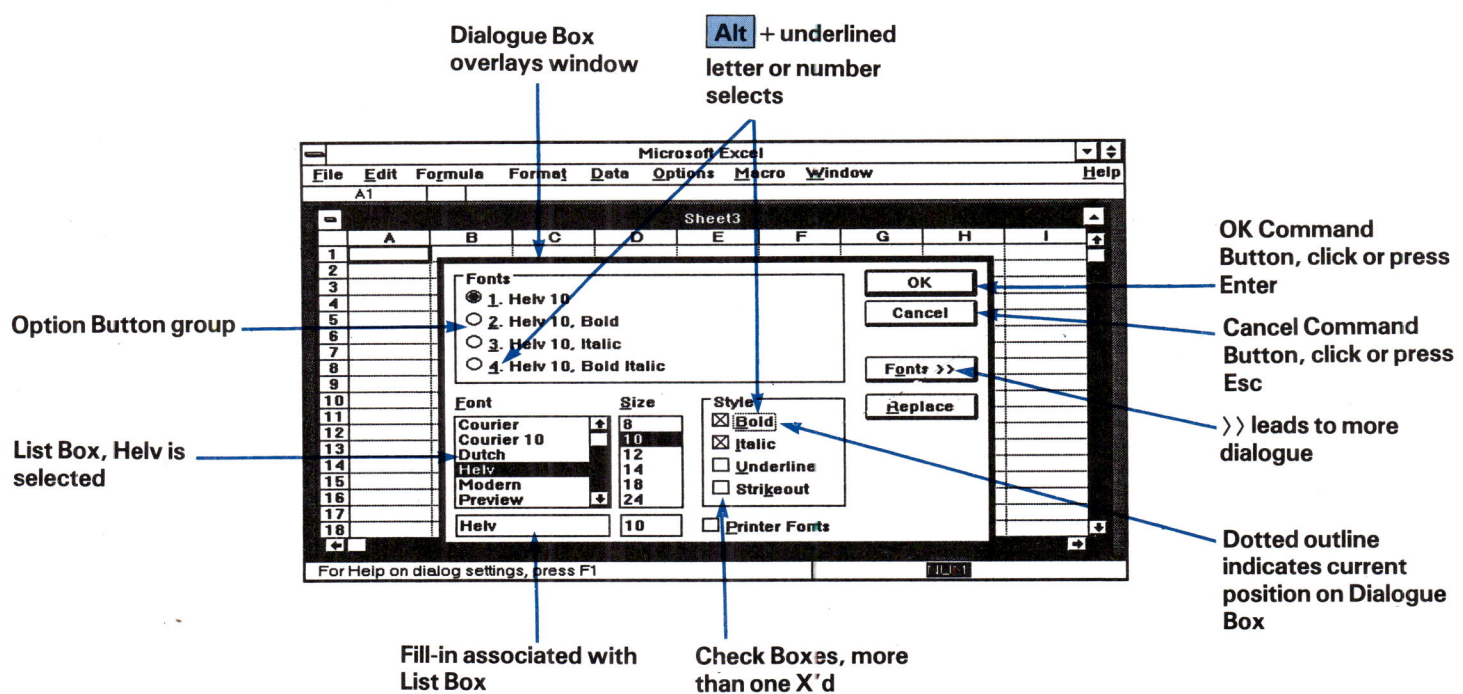

Dialogue Box overlays window

Alt + underlined letter or number selects

Option Button group

OK Command Button, click or press Enter

List Box, Helv is selected

Cancel Command Button, click or press Esc

〉〉 leads to more dialogue

Dotted outline indicates current position on Dialogue Box

Fill-in associated with List Box

Check Boxes, more than one X'd

5

The Worksheet

When you first load Excel you are presented with a blank worksheet ready for you to enter data.

Cells and ranges

The worksheet is divided into columns and rows which form a grid of *cells*. Each cell automatically has an address made up of the column letter and row number shown along the worksheet borders. For example, **A1** is the top left cell, while **G11** is at the intersection of the seventh column and eleventh row. Each cell can contain words, numbers or a calculation.

Some operations work on a group of adjacent cells, called a *range*. A range is addressed by its two diagonally opposite corners, separated by a colon. For example, **B2:E8** is a range that includes all the cells from column B row 2, at the top left, to column E row 8, at the bottom right.

Moving the Active Cell

Your worksheet appears on screen in a 'window' that is only big enough to reveal part of the sheet. The whole worksheet is 16,384 rows long and 256 columns wide. One cell is always surrounded by a thick border which can be moved about on screen. The bordered cell is called the *Active Cell*, the cell that is ready to receive your data. The Active Cell's address is displayed on the left in the line beneath the Menu Bar. Various key combinations provide shortcuts for moving the Active Cell around the worksheet:

Press	Move Active Cell
LeftArrow or **RightArrow**	One cell left or right.
UpArrow or **DownArrow**	One cell up or down.
Home	Column A of this row.
End	Rightmost column of this row containing data.
Ctrl+Home	To cell A1.
Ctrl+End	Bottom rightmost cell with data.
Ctrl+LeftArrow or **Ctrl+RightArrow**	Skip blocks of adjacent data, in this row.
Ctrl+UpArrow or **Ctrl+DownArrow**	Skip blocks of adjacent data, in this column.
F5	Go to specific cell.

Holding **Shift** with the above key combinations extends the selection over a range of cells instead of moving the Active Cell.

Screen prompts

The *Status Bar* is a line at the bottom of the screen that displays useful information about Excel's current task. The word 'Ready' appears there when Excel is waiting for you to enter data or choose from a menu. When choosing a command from the menu, look at the Status Bar to see a brief explanation of the command. The *Formula Bar* at the top of the worksheet displays the contents of the Active Cell as a formula without formatting.

Remember to check the Status and Formula Bars whenever you are having difficulty performing an operation.

The Worksheet

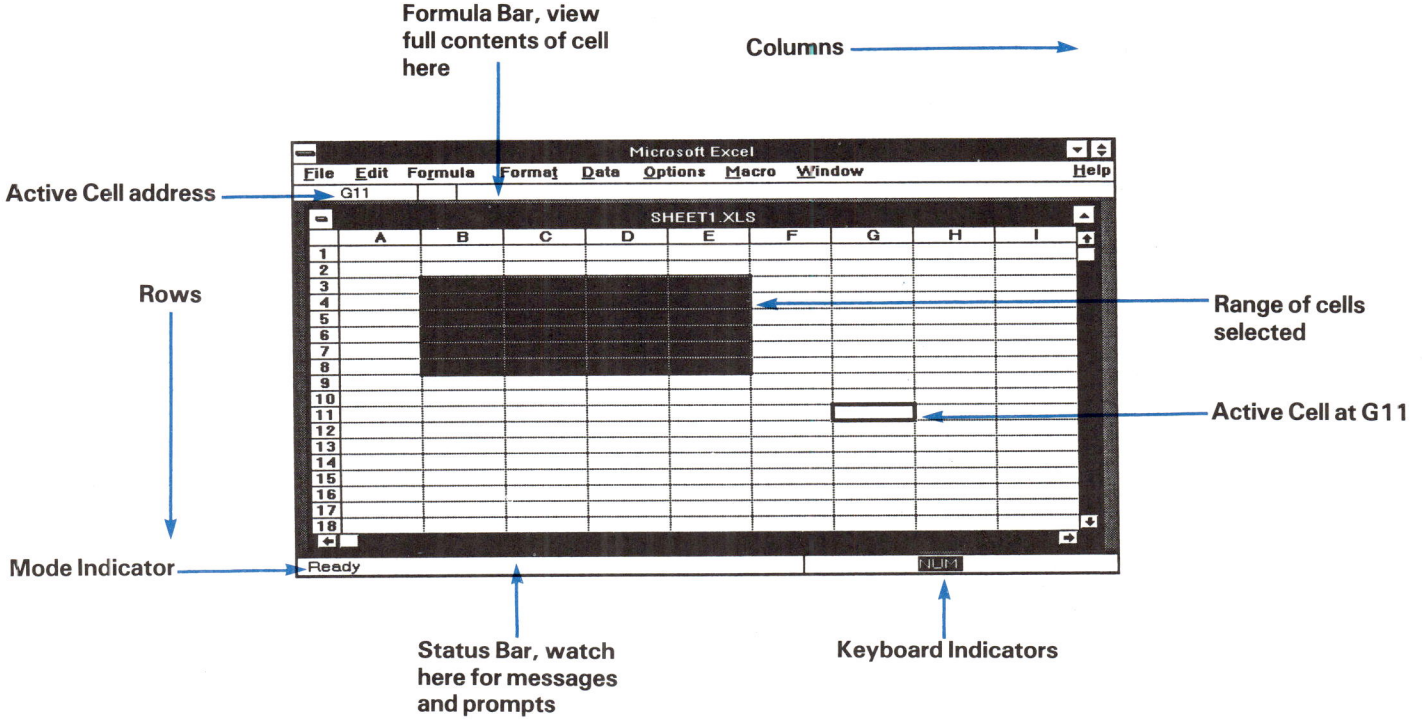

Formula Bar, view full contents of cell here

Columns

Active Cell address

Rows

Mode Indicator

Range of cells selected

Active Cell at G11

Status Bar, watch here for messages and prompts

Keyboard Indicators

Entering Data

Instructions

- Press **Ctrl+Home** to make sure that A1 is the active cell.
- Type a title such as *Trading Results*. Although the left part of the data temporarily disappears when the entry gets too wide for the active cell, the full entry appears in the formula bar just above the worksheet title. Press **Enter** to complete the entry.
- Press **DownArrow** twice until the active cell is in row three, then press **RightArrow** to move the pointer to column B. (Or with the mouse, click on B3.) The cell address B3 should appear in the reference area to the left of the formula bar.
- Type the label *Jan* as shown in the illustration, then press **Tab** to enter your typing and automatically advance to the adjacent cell, C3.
- Type the labels *Feb* in C3 and *Mar* in D3, pressing **Tab** between each entry.
- Select the cells A4, A5 and A6. Use the arrow keys to move the active cell to A4, press and hold the **Shift** key, use **DownArrow** to move to A6, then release the **Shift** key.
- Type the label *Revenue* in A4 then press **Enter** or **Tab**. Notice that the active cell moves to the next cell in the highlighted range automatically. Type *Costs* and *Profits* into A5 and A6.
- Save your work so far. Press **Alt** to activate the menu bar, **F** to choose File and then **A** to choose Save As. Type in a file name like *trade1*. The name you type will automatically replace any name which Excel has proposed, such as *sheet1*. Press **Enter** or click on **OK**.

Helpful tips

The appearance of the data can be improved later. See the example in *Changing Layout*.

To select a single cell with the mouse, position the mouse pointer over the cell then click. To select a range of cells, position the mouse pointer over the cell at one corner of the range, press and hold the left mouse button, drag the pointer to the diagonally opposite corner, then release the mouse button.

To correct an error while you are typing into a cell, use the **BackSpace** key to erase previous characters, or press **F2** to edit your entry so far. To correct a cell after you have left it, just type a new value into the cell or press **F2** to edit the existing contents. Use these keys to make corrections after pressing **F2**:

Press	Effect
Home	Move to the first character on the entry line.
End	Move to the last character on the entry line.
LeftArrow or **RightArrow**	Move one character in the direction of the arrow.
Ctrl+LeftArrow or **Ctrl+RightArrow**	Move one word in the direction of the arrow.
Backspace	Delete the previous character.
Delete	Delete character to the right of the insertion point.
Insert	Switch between inserting or overtyping characters. (The OVR Keyboard Indicator appears when overtyping.)
Esc	Return to the worksheet without change.
Enter	Accept the changes and return to the worksheet.

To clear a cell press **Ctrl+Delete** or press **Delete** and choose blanking options from the dialogue box.

To restore a cell to its previous value, use the undo feature. Press **Alt** then **E** to choose the Edit menu. Choose **U** for Undo. If you get the example totally wrong, select the entire worksheet using **Ctrl+Shift+Spacebar**, then press **Ctrl+Delete** to blank out all cells.

Saving a worksheet makes a permanent copy on disk which is essential in order to work with it again later.

Press **Alt, F, X** to leave Excel if you need to stop work now. Excel will ask you to save any unsaved work.

Entering Data

Ctrl + **Home** to make A1 the active cell

Type *Trading Results* then **↵**

↓ **↓** **→** to position at B3

Type *Jan* **Tab** and repeat for the other months

Position at A4 then **Shift** + **↓** twice

Type *Revenue* **↵** and repeat for *Costs* and *Profits*

Use arrow keys **→** **←** **↑** **↓** to position active cell

For corrections: Type new value over old, or press F2 to edit, or **Alt** + **Backspace** to undo

Contents of active cell apear in formula bar

Long text can spill into next cell

Labels align to left of cell

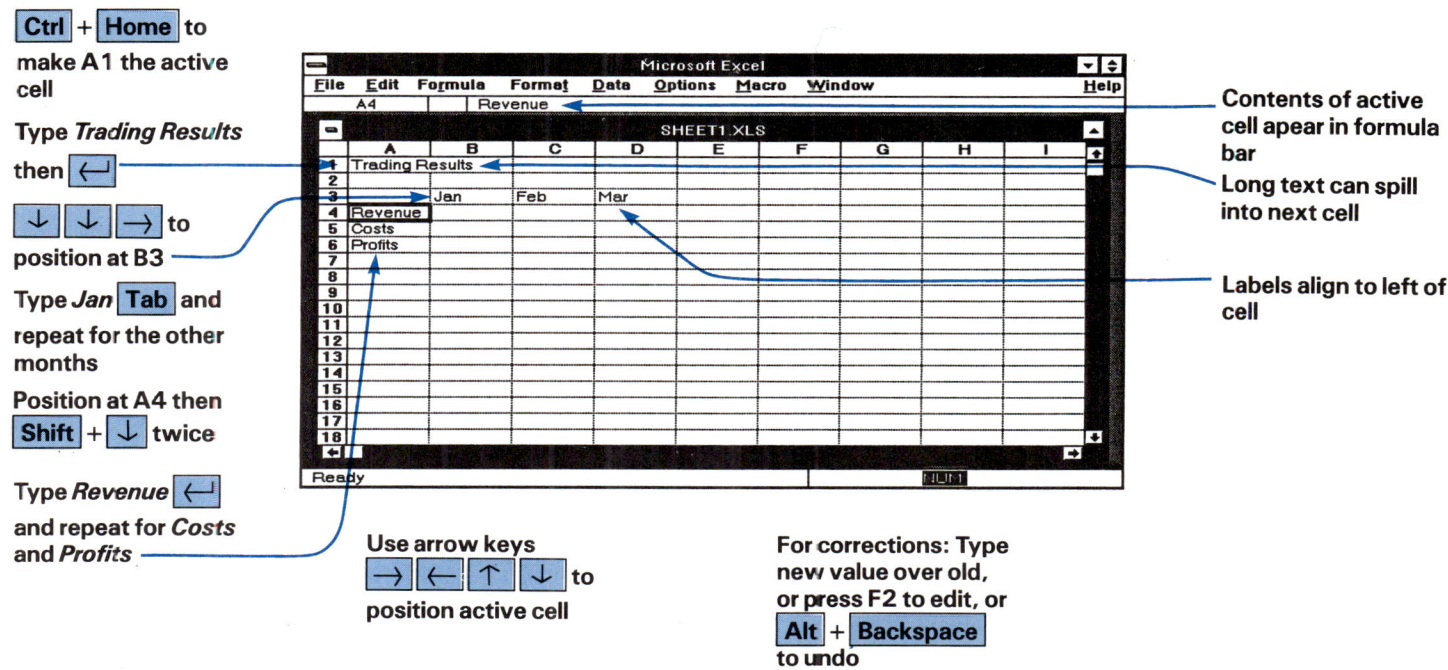

Alt **F** **A**

Type *trade1* over name Excel proposes

Press **↵** or click OK

Cell width and row heights are standard, but can be changed

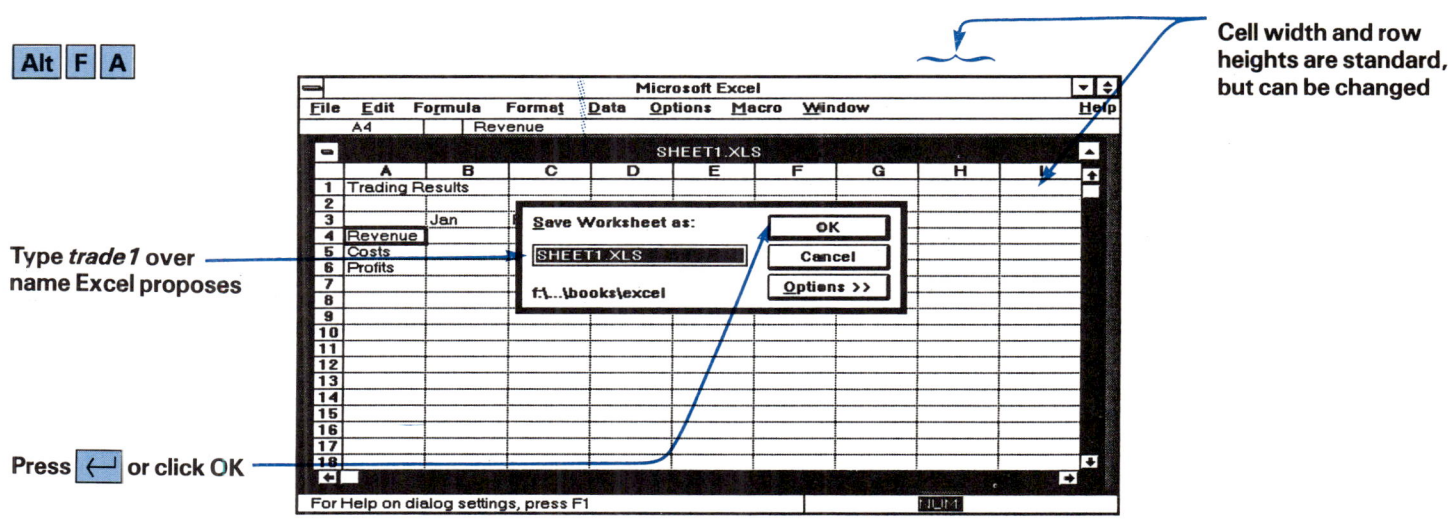

Using Formulas

The essence of the spreadsheet is that you can write a formula in one cell that calculates a result based on raw data entered in other cells. When you change the raw data, Excel automatically recalculates the formula and displays the updated result instantly.

Instructions

- Recall the *trade1* worksheet if it is not already on screen. Choose **Open** from the **File** menu. (**Alt, F, O**). When the dialogue box appears, type *trade1*, or press **Alt+F** to jump to the list of files, use the arrow keys or press the letter *t* until *trade1* is highlighted, then press **Enter**.
- Select the range B4 through D5. Type the figures shown in the illustration, pressing **Enter** or **Tab** between each entry.
- Use the arrow keys to move to B6 or click on B6 with the mouse.
- In B6 enter the formula =*B4-B5*. Notice that when you press **Enter** the cell displays the *results* of the formula, not the formula itself.
- To calculate the profits for the other months, copy the formula from B6 to columns C and D. With the active cell on B7, start the copy operation by choosing **Copy** from the **Edit** menu. (**Alt, E, C**). The active cell border flashes like a cinema marquee.
- Using the arrow keys or mouse, select cells C6 and D6.
- Press **Enter**. The formula is copied to each of the selected cells, and the marquee around B6 disappears indicating that the copy is complete.
- Check that the Profits are calculated correctly. If not, recheck your formula and data.
- Save the updated sheet. Choose **File, Save** (**Alt, F, S**) or press **Shift+F12**.
- In C5, type a new figure like *25000* and watch the screen as you press **Enter**. Changing the data, playing 'what if', doesn't harm the spreadsheet unless you type over a formula. Later examples show how to protect cells.

Helpful tips

As you type a value into a cell, Excel guesses what kind of data you're entering: a label, a number or a formula. The equals sign (=) before the cell reference B4 lets Excel distinguish between a formula and a label starting with the letter *B*.

A formula is a calculation using values stored in cells of the worksheet. When you copy a formula from one cell to another, Excel automatically adjusts the formula's cell references.

Excel can simplify data entry by advancing the active cell automatically. To get this effect, you select the cells you want to enter before typing in the data. Then after typing in each cell, press **Enter** or **Tab** to accept the entry and move to the next cell. After **Enter**, the active cell will automatically move down one row. After **Tab**, the active cell will move to the next column to the right. When you reach the edge of the selected range, Excel automatically advances to the next column or row. At the end of the entire selection, the active cell wraps back to the beginning of the range. To move quickly around the four corners of the selected range, press **Ctrl+.**

There is an alternative method for copying cells when the cells to copy from and to are contiguous in a row or column. First, select the cell with the formula to copy from *and* the adjacent cells to copy to. Then choose **Edit, Fill Right** (**Alt, E, H**) to copy to the right or **Edit, Fill Down** (**Alt, E, W**) to copy downwards.

You can continue working with a worksheet after it has been saved. If you want to remove the worksheet from screen to work on another project, choose **File, Close**. If the worksheet has changed since the last time you saved to disk, Excel gives you the chance to save (or lose) the changes.

Using Formulas

Alt **F** **O** *trade1* if worksheet is not still open

Use arrow keys to move active cell or click on B4

Shift + arrow key or drag to select B4:D5

Type *18000* ↵

Repeat for remaining figures

Type formula =*B4-B5* ↵ (Do not type 6000)

In B6, **Alt** **E** **C** select C6:D6, then ↵

Alt **F** **S** to re-save with changes

Move active cell to C5

Type *25000* over old figure

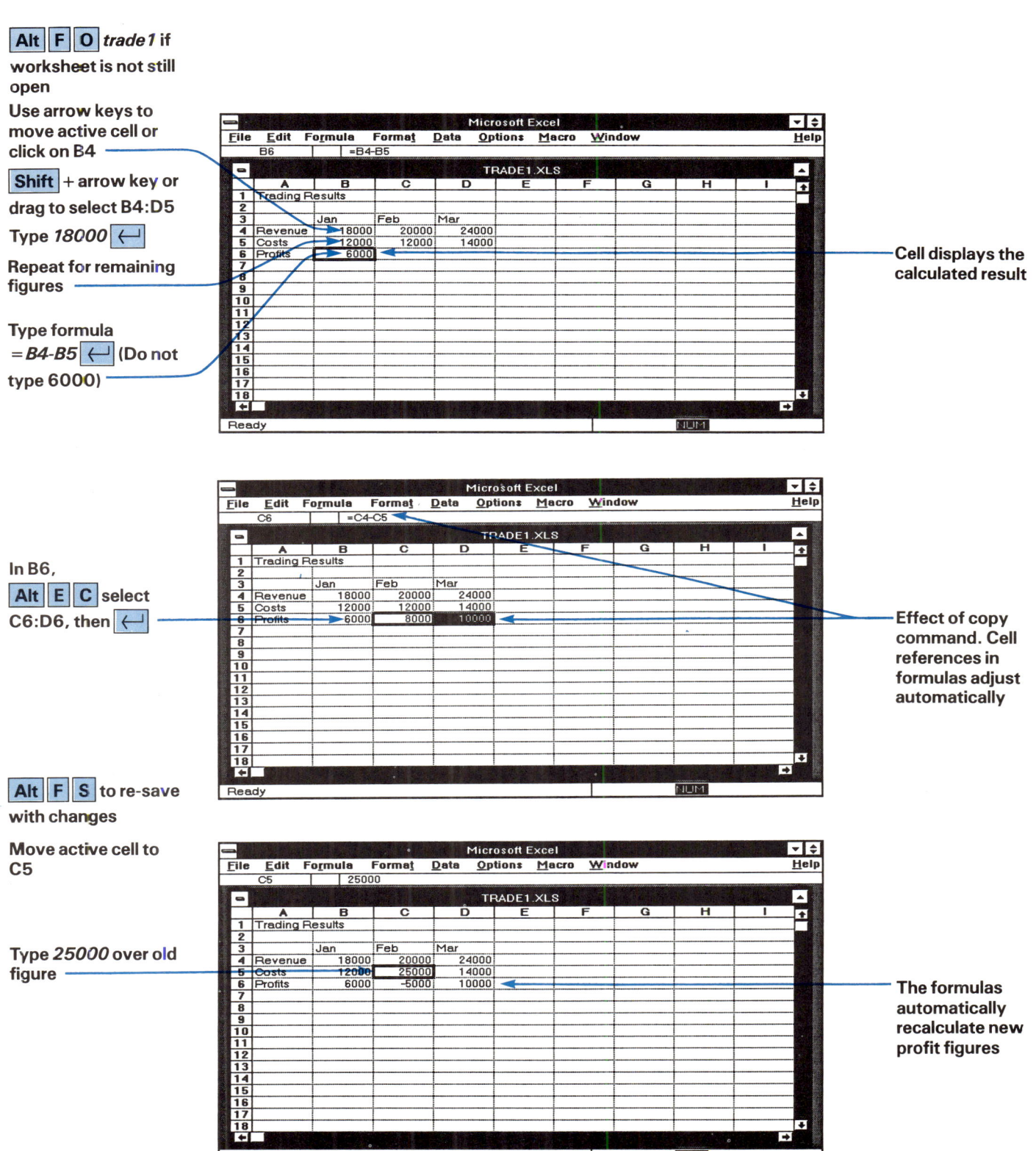

Cell displays the calculated result

Effect of copy command. Cell references in formulas adjust automatically

The formulas automatically recalculate new profit figures

Changing Layout

Many improvements can be made to the appearance of a worksheet to make it more readable and easier to understand. Changes to layout do not affect the raw data or results of calculations.

Instructions

- If it is not open, reload the *trade1* worksheet by choosing **File, Open**.
- Change the font to make the title stand out. Select cell A1. Choose **Format, Font**, pick a bold font from the choices on dialogue box (**Alt+2**), and press **Enter**.
- The names of the months would look better lined up with the right edge of the figures. Select the range B3 to D3. Choose **Format, Alignment**. The possible alignments appear in a dialogue box. Choose **Right (Alt+R)** and press **Enter**.
- Widen the column with the labels *Sales*, etc. Move the active cell to any cell in column A. Choose **Format, Column Width**. Type in a width of *11* and press **Enter**.
- Make it clearer that the figures represent money. Select B4:D6 and choose **Format, Number**. The dialogue box which appears has a list of possible formats for numbers. Press £ to choose the first format that begins with £ and press **Enter**.
- Borders would help the figures stand out from the month and account names. First to make it easy to see the borders, remove the gridlines from screen. Choose **Options, Display**, switch off **Gridlines** from the dialogue box and press **Enter**. Select A3 to D6. Then choose **Format, Border** and switch on **Outline** from the dialogue box.
- Select the top row of labels, A3:D3. Use the same technique as above to switch on a **Bottom** border. Select the bottom row of the data and switch on a **Top** border. Finally, select cells A3 to A6 and switch on a **Right** border.
- Choose **File, Save As** or press **F12** and type in a name like *trade2*.

Helpful tips

The Excel **Format, Number** command lists many choices for changing the appearance of numbers and dates. See the *Excel Reference* at the back of the book for the meaning of the format codes.

You can also apply changes in format to the whole worksheet, a whole column, several whole columns, a row or several rows by first selecting then formatting. Here are the keyboard and mouse procedures:

To Select	Keyboard	Mouse
Whole worksheet	**Ctrl+Shift+Spacebar**	Click in upper left corner of worksheet border.
Whole column	**Ctrl+Spacebar**	Click on column letter in worksheet border.
Several columns	Select cells in 1 row, then **Ctrl+Spacebar**	Drag across column letters in worksheet border.
Whole row	**Shift+Spacebar**	Click on row number in worksheet border.
Several rows	Select cells in 1 column, then **Shift+Spacebar**	Drag across row numbers in worksheet border.

Resizing a column or row is usually easier with the mouse. To resize a column or row, place the mouse pointer in the border between two columns or two rows until the mouse pointer changes shape, press the left mouse button then drag until the column or row is the desired size.

To reset a column or row to the normal size, switch on **Standard Size** on the **Format, Column Width** or **Format, Row Height** dialogue boxes.

Changing Layout

Alt F O *trade1* **if
worksheet is not still
open**

Ctrl + **Home** to
select A1, then
Alt T F Alt + **2**
to pick bold font

Select B3:D3, then
Alt T A Alt + **R**
**to align text to right
of cell**

**Move active cell to
column A, then**
Ctrl + **Spacebar** to
select column

Alt T C *11* ⏎ to
widen column

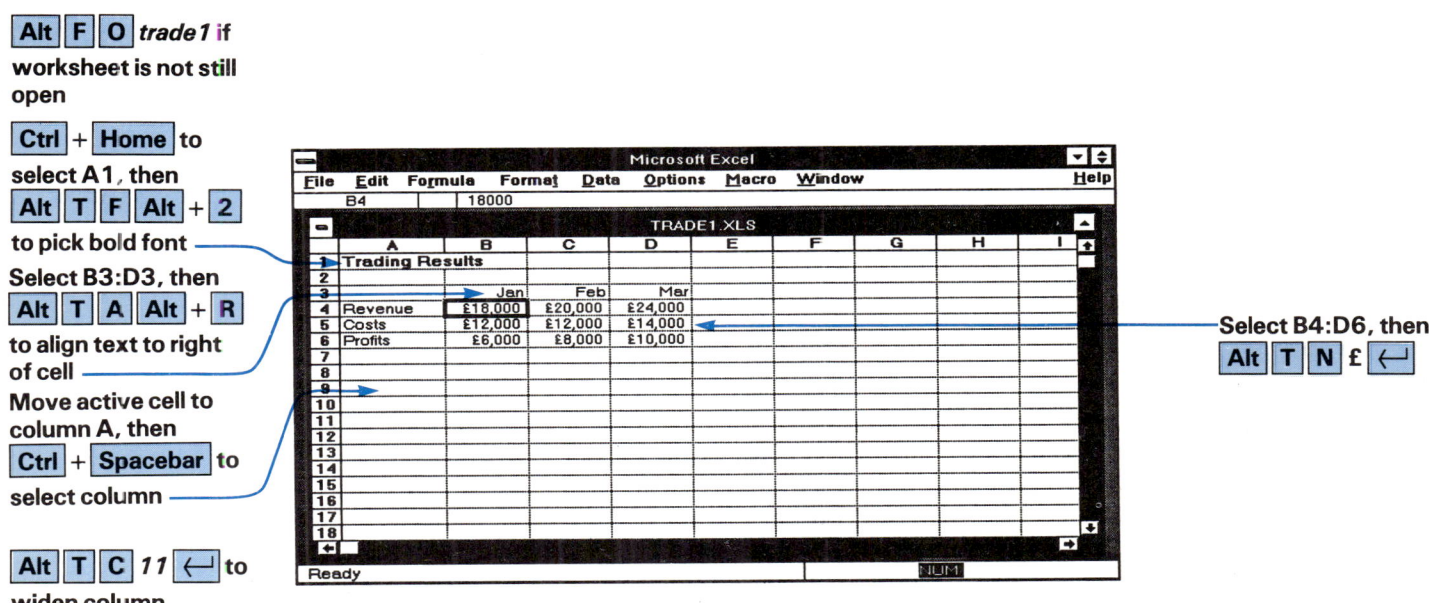

Select B4:D6, then
Alt T N £ ⏎

**Set up borders as
follows:**

Select A3:D6, then
Alt T B Alt + **O**

Select A3:D3, then
Alt T B Alt + **B**

Select A3:D3, then
Alt T B Alt + **T**

Select A3:A6, then
Alt T B Alt + **R**

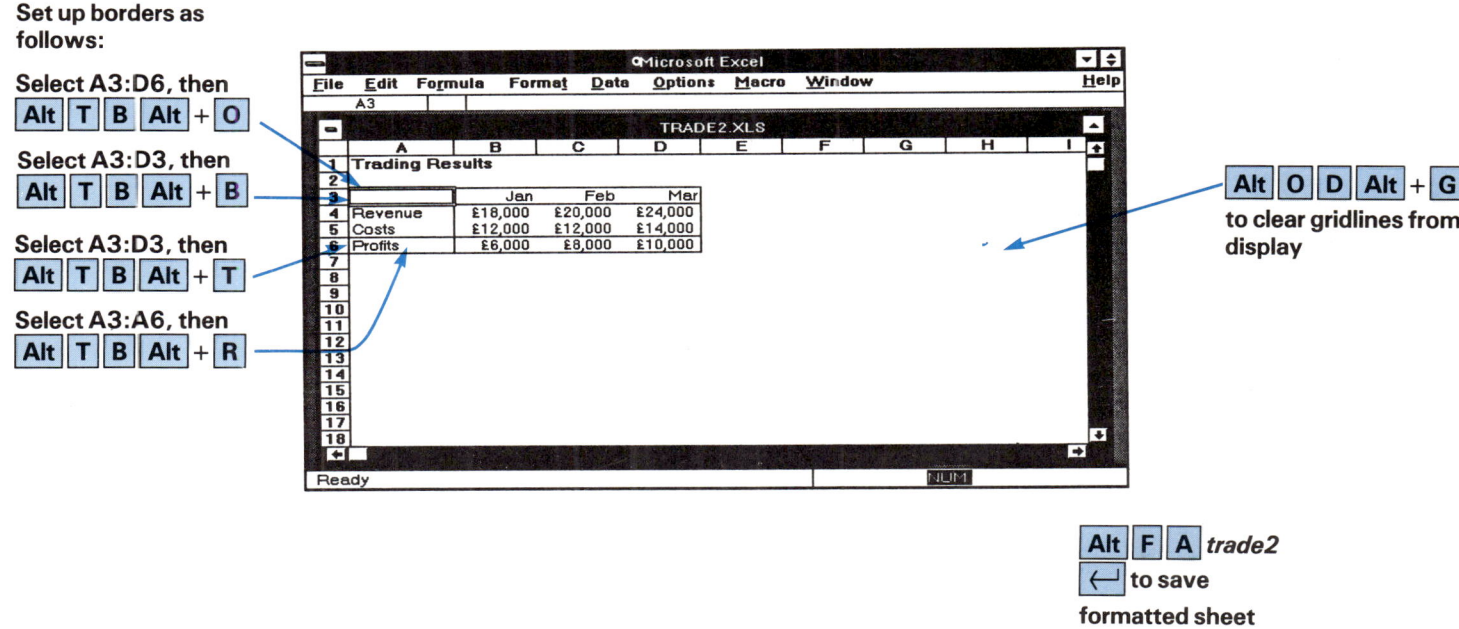

Alt O D Alt + **G**
**to clear gridlines from
display**

Alt F A *trade2*
⏎ **to save
formatted sheet
under a new name**

Simple Printing

Excel allows you to print a worksheet in draft or in final form which closely matches the worksheet's appearance on screen. Printing works in a way which allows you to continue working while your printer is printing. Excel prepares the report and sends it to another application called the Print Manager. The Print Manager takes care of sending the report to the printer while you get on with other work in Excel.

Instructions

- Load a worksheet like *trade2* from the previous example or one of your own choosing.
- Ensure that your printer is switched on and ready.
- Choose **File, Print** or press **Ctrl+Shift+F12**. Press **Enter** to accept the default printing options. Excel starts preparing the report for the Print Manager. Press **Esc** if you wish to stop Excel before it has finished preparing the report.
- It is possible to change the margins, headers and footers, and to print without the borders and gridlines. Choose **File, Page Setup**. Switch off **Gridlines** and **Row and Column Headings**. Modify margins as desired and press **Enter**.
- Print the report again. Choose **File, Print** or press **Ctrl+Shift+F12**. Press **Enter**.
- When you are happy with the printed output, re-save the worksheet to keep the changed page layout.

Helpful tips

By default, Excel prints out the entire worksheet. You can print selected parts of the worksheet by selecting a range of cells and choosing **Options, Set Print Area**.

Page size and orientation (long or wide) are set from the **Printer Setup** item on the **File** menu.

You can see a preview of how the printed page will look by choosing **File, Print** and then switching on the **Preview** option.

To print formulas instead of calculated results, choose **Options, Display** and switch on the **Formulas** option. Then print as normal.

There are numerous ways of enhancing an Excel report. See the illustration pages entitled *Enhancing Printouts*.

If you do not get the printout you expect, check that your printer is correctly installed in the Excel and Windows environments. First, check the configuration of the printer by choosing **Printer Setup** from the **File** menu. If the configuration is correct but you still do not get output, you may need to run the Control Panel application. To run Control Panel, press **Alt+Spacebar** to pull down the Excel Application Menu, choose **Run** and pick **Control Panel**. Choose **Printers** on the Control Panel and make sure that your printer is shown as active.

If a printer problem occurs while sending your report to the printer, such as the printer runs out of paper, the Print Manager pops up a message box over your worksheet. Press **Enter** to acknowledge the message. When it becomes convenient to interrupt your work in Excel, fix the problem with the printer (for example, add paper) then switch to the Print Manager to resume printing. To switch between Excel and the Print Manager, press **Ctrl+Esc** to see the list of programs running. Choose **Print Manager** and press **Enter**. Choose **Resume** in the Print Manager, then switch back to Excel.

If you have the run time version of Windows before Windows 3.0, the Spooler performs a similar function to the Print Manager.

Simple Printing

Alt **F** **O** *trade2* if worksheet is not still open

Check that printer is switched on and is 'on-line'

Screen

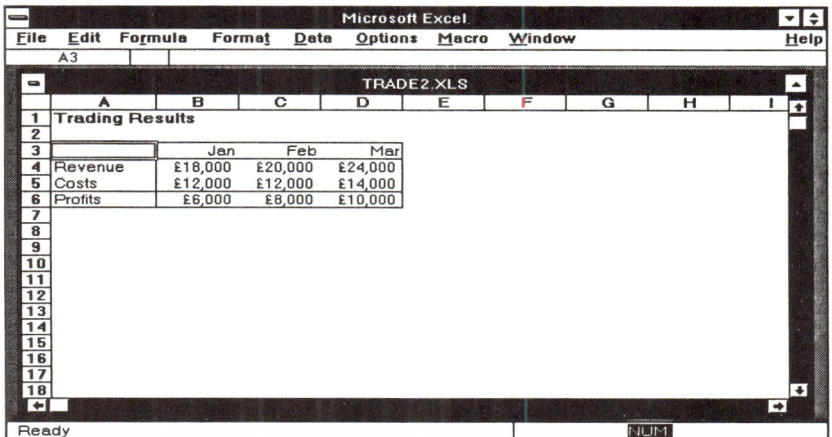

Paper

Alt **F** **P** ⏎ to send report to Print Manager

	A	B	C	D
1	Trading Results			
2				
3		Jan	Feb	Mar
4	Revenue	£18,000	£20,000	£24,000
5	Costs	£12,000	£12,000	£14,000
6	Profits	£6,000	£8,000	£10,000

Paper

Printout without borders and gridlines

Alt **F** **T** **Alt** + **G** **Alt** + **C** to clear grid and borders from printout

Alt **F** **P** ⏎ to send report

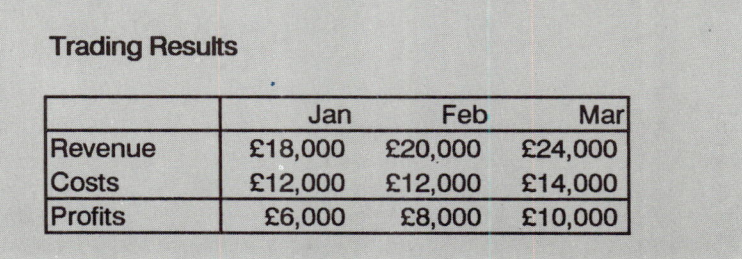

Trading Results

	Jan	Feb	Mar
Revenue	£18,000	£20,000	£24,000
Costs	£12,000	£12,000	£14,000
Profits	£6,000	£8,000	£10,000

Simple Graphing

Presenting data graphically is one of the major attractions of a spreadsheet program. This illustration concentrates on Excel's clever automatic charting features.

Instructions

- Retrieve *trade1* or a similar worksheet and close any others in the workspace.
- Select the range A3 to D6.
- Choose **File, New** and pick the **Chart** option from the dialogue box. Press **Enter**. Excel places a chart window over the worksheet window.
- Notice that the menu bar at the top of the screen has changed. Also, Excel has automatically labelled each category along the bottom, X-axis, with the names of the months taken from the worksheet.
- Place the worksheet and chart side by side: choose **Window, Arrange All**.
- Switch back to the worksheet window by clicking anywhere on the worksheet or by pressing **Ctrl+F6**. Change the amount in cell D5 to *8000*. Watch the chart change.
- Switch back to the chart window (**Ctrl+F6**) and maximise the chart (**Ctrl+F10**).
- To identify the columns for each month, a legend is needed. From the new menu bar, choose **Chart**, then **Add Legend**. Excel automatically uses the labels in column to the left of the data as the legend.
- Add a title to complete the chart. Choose **Chart, Attach Text**, then pick **Chart Title** from the dialogue box and press **Enter**. Excel inserts the word 'Title' surrounded by small boxes called handles which indicate that the title is selected. Press **F2** to edit the title in the formula bar. Backspace over 'Title', type *Trading Results* instead and press **Enter**. Click on a blank part of the chart to remove the handles.
- Print the chart from the **File, Print** menu.
- Save the chart and worksheet together as a *workspace*. Choose **Save Workspace** from the **File** menu. Excel prompts you to name and save the workspace, the new chart and the changed worksheet. Replace the workspace and chart names proposed by Excel with something more identifiable.

Helpful tips

Excel chooses how to arrange a chart based on the shape of the selection on the worksheet. The wide side of the selection becomes the basis of the categories along the X-axis of the chart.

Use the **Gallery** menu to change the kind of graph which Excel displays. Excel uses the term Bar chart for horizontal bars and the term Column chart for vertical bars. The Column chart is the default chart type.

You can control the size and shape of the printed chart by sizing the chart window on screen and selecting option on the **File, Page Setup** menu. It is easiest to size the window by stretching its borders using the mouse until it has the proportions you want. Then choose **File, Page Setup**. Pick one of the size options. **Screen Size** is self-explanatory. **Fit to Page** makes the chart as large as possible without changing the proportions. **Full Page** prints the chart as large as possible.

The workspace, chart and worksheet in the example could all have the same file name, *trade1*. Excel adds a unique extension to each type of document: XLS for a worksheet, XLC for a chart and XLW for the workspace.

More information on customising charts is presented in the pages entitled *Enhancing Graphs*.

Simple Graphing

Source Worksheet

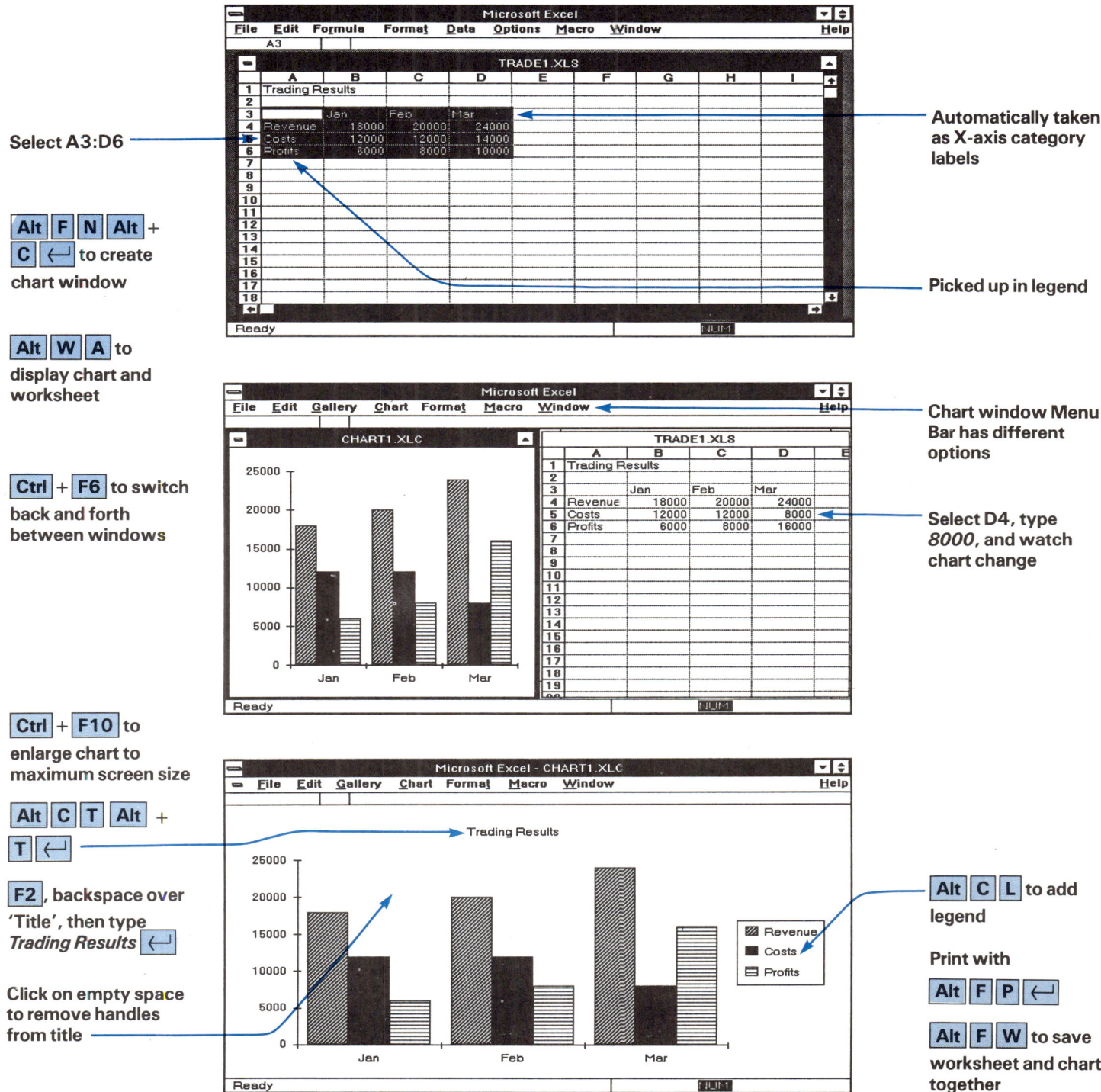

Select A3:D6

Automatically taken as X-axis category labels

`Alt` `F` `N` `Alt` +
`C` `↵` to create
chart window

Picked up in legend

`Alt` `W` `A` to
display chart and
worksheet

Chart window Menu Bar has different options

`Ctrl` + `F6` to switch
back and forth
between windows

Select D4, type
8000, and watch
chart change

`Ctrl` + `F10` to
enlarge chart to
maximum screen size

`Alt` `C` `T` `Alt` +
`T` `↵`

`F2`, backspace over
'Title', then type
Trading Results `↵`

`Alt` `C` `L` to add
legend

Print with

`Alt` `F` `P` `↵`

Click on empty space
to remove handles
from title

`Alt` `F` `W` to save
worksheet and chart
together

Safeguards

This example illustrates some of the precautions you can take to prevent accidental or unauthorised changes to your worksheets. One technique helps spot errors when calculations have been incorrectly keyed. The other technique physically locks out any attempts to change the data.

Instructions

- Open the *trade1* worksheet.
- In cell E3, type *Total*.
- Select the range E4 to E6.
- Use the **SUM** function in cell E4 to sum up the Revenue for January through February. Type =*sum(B4:D4)* and press **Enter**.
- In the same range, replicate the formula in the rest of the range using **Edit, Fill Down**.
- Introduce a check total which calculates the Total Profits by another method and displays the difference, if any. Type *Check* in F8. In E8, type the formula =*E4-E5-E6*. If your worksheet is correct, E8 should display zero.
- Try out the check. Type over the formula in cell B6 with the value *4000*. Notice that the check cell contains a number other than zero. Restore the formula in B6 using **Edit, Undo**.
- Prepare to switch on worksheet 'protection'. First, select the raw data area, cells B4 to D5. Choose **Format, Cell Protection**, switch off **Locked** on the dialogue box, and press **Enter**. This keeps these cells unlocked when you turn on protection in the next instruction.
- Turn on protection using **Options, Protect Document**, switch on **Contents**, and press **Enter**.
- Notice the difference when typing over B7 which is locked and B4 which you unlocked.
- Save the worksheet under a new name such as *trade3* using **File, Save As**.

Helpful tips

Functions are formulas built into Excel that save you having to type in long and complex calculations. For example, **SUM** is a function that saves entering a whole list of individual figures separated by plus signs. Excel has dozens more functions for financial, scientific and other applications. When entering a function in a cell, choose **Formula, Paste Function** to see a list of Excel's functions.

Excel calculates correctly so why use a check cell? It's surprisingly easy to type over a cell containing a formula. This leads to worksheets that look right until you actually check the results. Businesses have failed because of incorrect or accidentally corrupted formulas in worksheets.

Use **Options, Unprotect Document** to switch off protection if you need to modify a protected cell.

Excel contains other, more stringent security measures. Prevent others from unprotecting the document by assigning a password when you protect the document using **Options, Protect Document**. Next time you or anyone attempts to unprotect the document, Excel will ask you for the password. **Don't forget it!**

Prevent others from reading a file at all by assigning it a password when you save it. Choose **File, Save** or **Save As, Options, Password**. Fill in the password. Next time you or anyone attempts to **Open** the file, Excel will ask you for the file password which can be different than the document protection password. **Don't forget the password!**

Safeguards

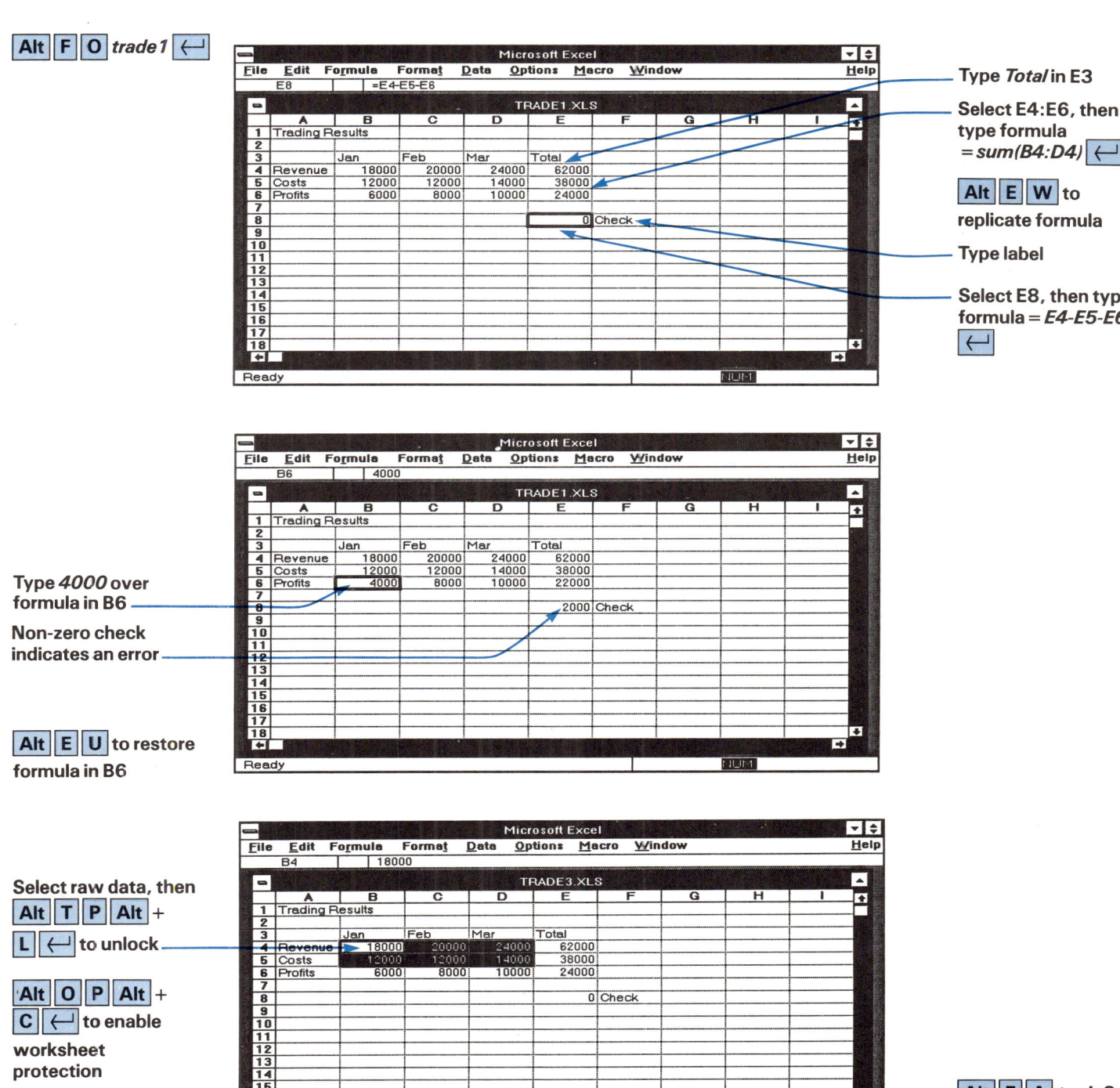

`Alt` `F` `O` *trade1* `↵`

Type *Total* in E3

Select E4:E6, then type formula = *sum(B4:D4)* `↵`

`Alt` `E` `W` to replicate formula

Type label

Select E8, then type formula = *E4-E5-E6* `↵`

Type *4000* over formula in B6

Non-zero check indicates an error

`Alt` `E` `U` to restore formula in B6

Select raw data, then `Alt` `T` `P` `Alt` + `L` `↵` to unlock

`Alt` `O` `P` `Alt` + `C` `↵` to enable worksheet protection

`Alt` `F` `A` *trade3* `↵` to save under a new name

Viewing

Excel provides features that simplify working with worksheets that are too big to fit on a screen. You can divide the worksheet window into 'panes' or display the same worksheet in several windows at once.

Instructions

- Build a worksheet like the one shown (*trade1* with figures for April to September.)
- Press **Ctrl+End** to move the active cell to the lower rightmost cell of the sheet. Notice that the row headings in column A are no longer visible.
- To keep column or row headings visible: First, press **Ctrl+Home** to jump back to A1. Next, split the window into panes. Pull down the Document menu with **Alt, Hyphen** and choose **Split**. Move the shaded lines with the arrow keys or mouse until the vertical shadow is between columns A and B and the horizontal shadow is between rows 3 and 4. Press **Enter**. Finally, choose **Options, Freeze Panes**.
- Press **Ctrl+End** and notice that column A is still visible but column B has disappeared.
- Choose **Options, Unfreeze Panes** and experiment with moving around the worksheet. Press **F6** or **Shift+F6** to jump from pane to pane.
- To revert to a single pane, choose **Alt, Hyphen, Split**, then use the arrow keys or mouse to move the shaded lines off the worksheet.
- You can display the same worksheet in more than one window at a time. Choose **Window, New Window**. Your sheet appears in a second window that covers most of your first window. Choose **Window, Arrange All** to display both windows side-by-side.
- Experiment with moving around the active window. Press **Ctrl+F6** or **Shift+Ctrl+F6** to jump windows. Make a change to a cell. Satisfy yourself that the change appears in both windows.
- To close a window, choose **Alt, Hyphen, Close**. Choose **Window, Arrange All** to quickly resize the remaining open window to full size.

Helpful tips

Use frozen panes to keep column and row headings in view. Unfrozen panes are most useful with two panes instead of four, particularly with large databases. Use multiple windows to work totally independently on different parts of the same sheet – each window has its own active cell.

The following keys move the active cell over the worksheet in big jumps:

Press	Move Active Cell
PageUp or **PageDown**	One screenful up or down.
Ctrl+PageUp or **Ctrl+PageDown**	One screenful left or right

Using the movement keys with **ScrollLock** turned on moves the window over the spreadsheet without moving the active cell.

To move in large jumps with the mouse, scroll the worksheet by clicking on the horizontal or vertical scroll bars at the bottom and right of the window.

To get the biggest possible view of a worksheet on screen, maximise it. Press **Ctrl+F10** or choose **Maximize** from the Document menu (**Alt, Hyphen**). There are subtle changes to the screen when a worksheet is maximised. Most noticeable is that there is only one title bar on the screen, and it displays the name of the worksheet or chart instead of 'Microsoft Excel'.

Press **Ctrl+F5** or choose **Restore** from the Document menu to reduce the window back to its original size.

Viewing

Add figures for April
to September to a
sheet like *trade1*

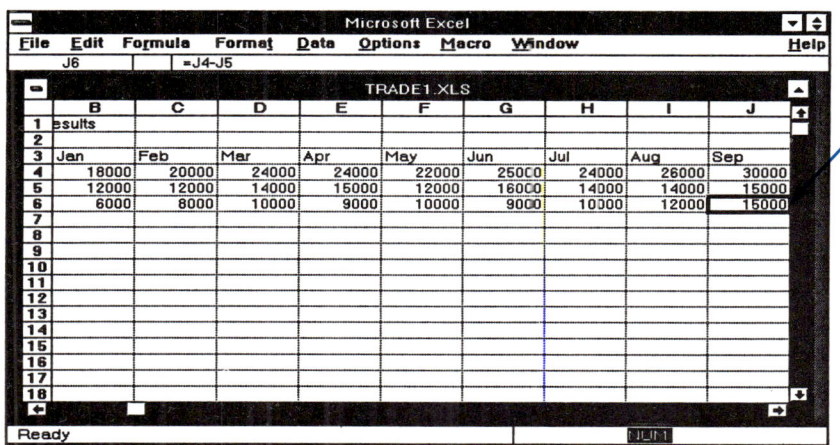

Ctrl + **End** to jump
to last cell on sheet.
Column A disappears

Ctrl + **Home** to A1

Alt **Hyphen** **T** to
start split operation
Use arrow keys or
mouse to position
split, then **↵**

Alt **O** **F** to freeze
panes

Alt **O** **F** to
unfreeze panes

Alt **Hyphen** **T**,
then use arrow keys
or mouse to pull split
lines off window

Ctrl + **End** to jump
to last cell. Column B
disappears

F6 and **Shift** + **F6**
to move to next pane

Alt **W** **N** to create
a second window for
the same sheet

Alt **W** **A** to
view both windows
side-by-side

Ctrl + **F6** and
Shift + **Ctrl** + F6
to move between
windows

Alt **Hyphen** **C** to
close a window

Alt **W** **A** to re-size
remaining window

Cash Forecast

Cash flow forecasting is a typical worksheet application. This example shows a basic technique for rolling the cash position forward from month to month.

Instructions

- Select column A, and widen it to 15 using **Format, Column Width**.
- Type in the labels in column A and in row 3. Use **Format, Alignment, Right** to arrange the month names over the numbers which will be entered in the columns.
- Beginning with February, the *Brought Fwd* from one month is derived from the *In Hand* at the end of the previous month. In cell C4 enter the formula $=B18$.
- Select the range C4 to G4 and choose **Edit, Fill Right** to copy the formula to the rest of the Brought Forward row.
- The formulas in column B in the first illustration calculate the cash position for the month then add it to the amount brought forward. Enter the formulas shown in cells B8, B14, B16 and B18.
- Select the range B8 to G18. Use **Edit, Fill Right** to copy the formulas to the other months.
- Use **Format, Cell Protection** and switch off **Locked** to unlock the data entry areas. Then switch on protection using **Options, Protect Document**.
- Save your model without figures under a name such as *cashflow*.
- Type in your income and expenditure figures.
- Use **File, Save As** to save the filled in forecast under a different name such as *cash1*.
- Print out your work using **File, Print**.
- Clear the workspace to work on another project using **File, Close**.

Helpful tips

To display formulas instead of values, choose **Options, Display**, switch on **Formulas** and press **Enter**. Or use the shortcut, **Ctrl+Apostrophe**. Cells automatically widen to accomodate formulas which are usually longer than values.

Every time you make an entry in a cell, Excel recalculates some or all of the formulas on the worksheet. Use **Options, Calculation, Manual** to switch to manual recalculation. If you change a value on the worksheet which affects other values, 'Calculation' appears in the Status Bar at the bottom of the screen. You can continue entering data but don't rely on the results displayed. Press **F9** or **Ctrl+Equals** when you want Excel to recalculate the sheet. Use **Options, Calculation, Automatic** to resume automatic recalculation.

Excel is optimised to recalculate only the formulas affected by a change. It does this 'in the background' while you continue working.

When the value of a formula in a cell depends on itself, directly or indirectly, your worksheet is said to contain a *circular reference*. Usually this is an error which happens accidentally. For example, type $=G18$ in cell B4. Excel displays a dialogue box to which you must reply OK. Note that 'Circular' appears in the Status Bar.

Sometimes a circular reference is intentional. Excel needs to recalculate the whole sheet several times to converge on a result. The number of iterations is controlled using **Options, Calculation, Iteration**.

Cash Forecast

Formula Display

Move active cell to column A, then
`Alt` `T` `C` *15* `←`

Type labels in column A and row 3

Enter formulas shown in column B

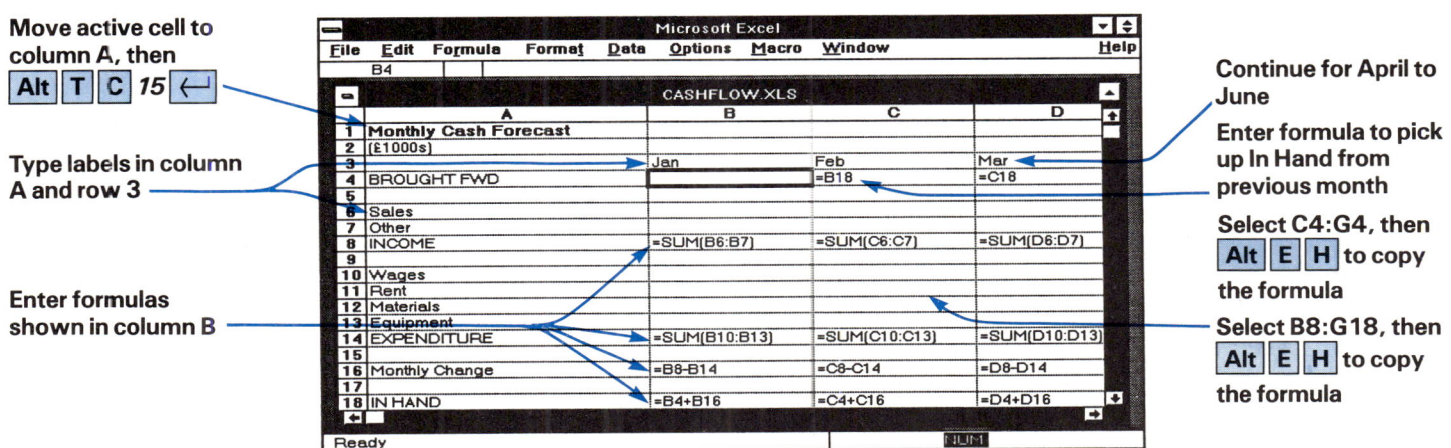

Continue for April to June

Enter formula to pick up In Hand from previous month

Select C4:G4, then `Alt` `E` `H` to copy the formula

Select B8:G18, then `Alt` `E` `H` to copy the formula

Final Display

Unlock data entry areas with `Alt` `T` `P`
`Alt` + `L` `←`

Switch on worksheet protection with
`Alt` `O` `P`

Save model with
`Alt` `F` `A` *cashflow*
`←`

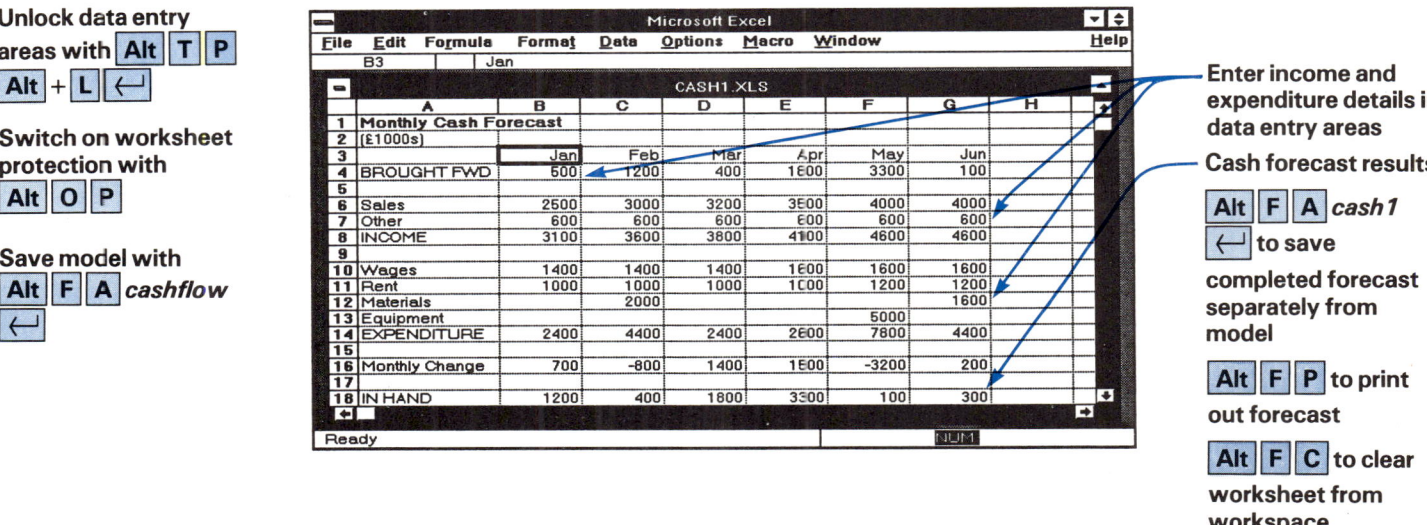

Enter income and expenditure details in data entry areas

Cash forecast results

`Alt` `F` `A` *cash1*
`←` to save completed forecast separately from model

`Alt` `F` `P` to print out forecast

`Alt` `F` `C` to clear worksheet from workspace

Invoice

Here is an example of how you might prepare the different parts of an invoice with VAT automatically calculated. Discounts could be handled in a similar way.

Instructions

- Open a new worksheet.
- Type in the labels as shown on the first illustration. Enter the VAT rates in D15 to D17 as shown with the percent sign.
- The Amount will be the product of Quantity and Price. Select G8 to G12. In G8, type in the formula =*E8*F8*, then choose **Edit, Fill Down** to copy the formula.
- When you fill in the invoice, you will type in a VAT code in the Code column. The formula in column I uses the Excel **VLOOKUP** function to find the code in the table at the bottom of the invoice, pick the corresponding VAT rate, and calculate the VAT. Select I8 to I12, type in the formula shown on the illustration, then copy the formula to the rest of the selection.
- Type in the formulas to add up the Sub-total, VAT, and Total in cells G14, G15 and G16.
- Using **Format, Cell Protection**, unlock the data entry areas: B3 to B5 for Client name and address; I3 to I5 for Date, Invoice number, and Account number; A8 to B12 for Item number and Description; E8 to F12 for Quantity and Price; and H8 to H12 for VAT Code. Then switch on protection with **Options, Protect Document**.
- Type in the data shown on the illustration. With protection on, you will not be able to type over the calculated cells which are locked.
- Notice that the amounts keyed in and calculated all display with different numbers of decimal places. Format the amounts in column F, G and I. Choose **Format, Number** to see the built-in Excel formats, and pick **0.00**.
- Now the amounts all display in pounds and pence, but notice that the VAT does not appear to add up correctly. Choose **Options, Calculation, Precision as Displayed** to tell Excel to ignore any decimal places beyond those displayed.

Helpful tips

Excel automatically understands numbers entered as percents, for example, 15% is used as .15 in a calculation.

To enter the **VLOOKUP** function, choose **Formula, Paste Function** to see the list of Excel functions. Press *V* repeatedly until **VLOOKUP** is selected, and press **Enter**.

The range of the VAT rate table in the **VLOOKUP** formula is defined using absolute references, but you don't need to type them in. To convert an address to an absolute references, type the address as usual, then press **F4**.

Although you reformat a field such as the calculated VAT to show only two decimal places, Excel stores the true figure with much greater accuracy. The hidden accuracy can cause an anomaly when you sum up the VAT. The total VAT displayed can be pennies out. To ensure that your sums display correctly, use **Precision as Displayed** as mentioned above. Alternatively, you can use the **ROUND** function to control how accurately calculated results are stored.

Use fonts, borders and alignments to improve the appearance of the invoice.

Excel has a wide variety of built-in formats for displaying numbers. Experiment with the formats on the **Format, Number** dialogue box to see how they effect the appearance of data in a cell.

Invoice

Enter labels as shown

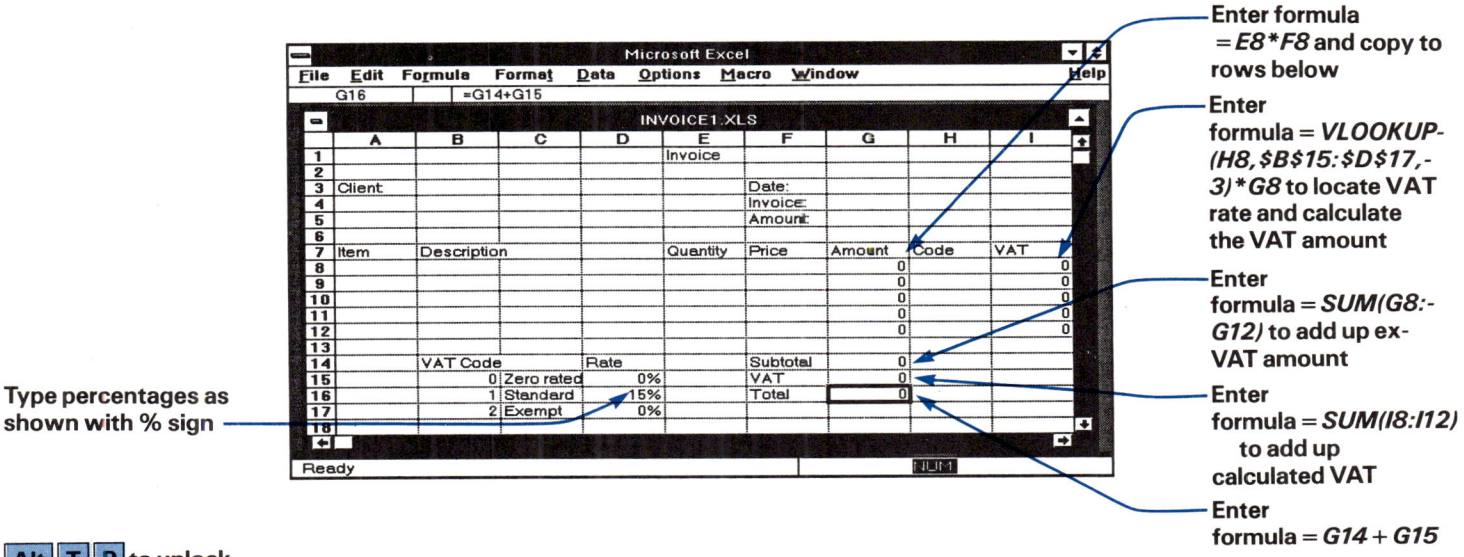

Enter formula
= *E8*F8* and copy to
rows below

Enter
formula = *VLOOKUP-
(H8,$B$15:$D$17,-
3)*G8* to locate VAT
rate and calculate
the VAT amount

Enter
formula = *SUM(G8:-
G12)* to add up ex-
VAT amount

Enter
formula = *SUM(I8:I12)*
to add up
calculated VAT

Enter
formula = *G14 + G15*

**Type percentages as
shown with % sign**

Alt **T** **P** to unlock
data entry areas

**Switch on worksheet
protection with
Alt O P**

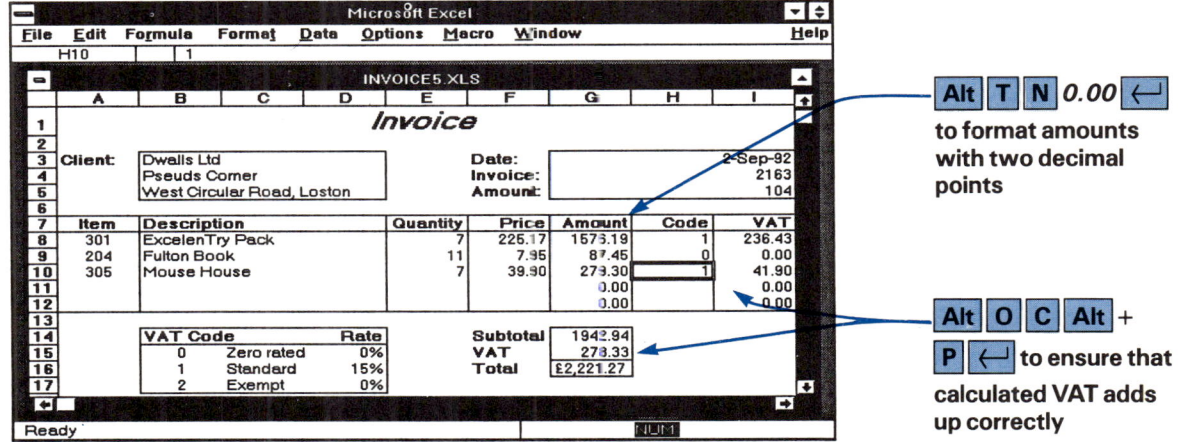

Alt **T** **N** *0.00* ←
to format amounts
with two decimal
points

Alt O C Alt +
P ← to ensure that
calculated VAT adds
up correctly

**Polish appearance
with borders,
alignment, fonts etc.
on Format menu**

Database

Excel's database features let you organise, store and retrieve lists of data.

Instructions

Sorting

- Type in the data shown in the first illustration.
- Place the active cell in column A and select the range A4 to C15, the data *without* the titles.
- Choose **Data, Sort**, then press **Enter** to accept column A as the sort key and ascending sequence for the output. Excel sorts the selected columns and rows.

Finding with a data form

- Select the range A3 to C15, the data *including* the titles in row 3. Choose **Data, Set Database** to identify this data as a database.
- Choose **Form** from the **Data** menu to display a data entry form on a dialogue box. Choose **Criteria**, then **Tab** to County, type in *Middx*, and press the **Find Next** command button (**Alt+N**). Excel shows you the first record which meets the criterion of being in Middlesex.
- Press **Find Next** again to see the next record which meets the criterion, or press **Find Prev** to see the previous match. Press the **Exit** command button to close the data form.

Finding and extracting

- Type in the *Criterion* area shown in the third illustration. Select the range F3 to H4, and choose **Data, Set Criteria** to define the search criteria for a find or extract operation.
- Choose **Data, Find**. Excel jumps to the first record in the database which meets the criteria. Press **DownArrow** to find the next record or **UpArrow** to find the previous. Press **Esc** to stop searching.
- Select F10 to H10 and type in the *Sales, Name* and *County* headings shown in the third illustration.
- With the range still highlighted, choose **Data, Extract**, then **Enter** to accept the dialogue box settings unchanged. Excel selects records which match the criteria, copies them from the database to the extract area, and arranges the fields under the headings in the extract area.

Helpful tips

Any part of a worksheet can be used as a database. Keep in mind that you need column headings for **Data Form, Find**, or **Extract** operations.

When you sort a database you lose its original order. If you make a mistake, use **Edit Undo** immediately after a sort to restore the original order.

A Data Form can also be used to add, change or delete records from the database.

Use wildcard characters ? and * in criteria fields to do 'fuzzy' searches. A question mark matches any character in that specific position. An asterisk matches any group of characters. Try *S** to extract Sussex and Surrey or *S?r** to extract only Surrey.

You can fill in more than one column in a row of the criteria area and you can have more than one row of criteria. If a record matches all of the criteria on any single row, it will be selected.

You can use formulas as criteria. To select all records with sales over £500, enter ⟩500 under Sales in the criteria area.

Database

27

Sorting

Enter data as shown

Select A4:C15 (Do not select titles in A3)

Alt **D** **S** **↵** to sort

Data Form

Select A3:C15, then

Alt **D** **B** to set up database

Alt **D** **O** to display data entry form

Alt + **C** **Tab** *Middx*

Alt + **N** to find first

Alt + **N** to find next,

Alt + **P** to find previous

Alt + **X** to finish

Data Management

Enhance sheet with CRITERIA area

Select F3:H4, then

Alt **D** **C**

Alt **D** **F** for first find

↓ or **↑** for further finds, **Esc** to finish

Select F10:H10 and type heading exactly as shown

Alt **D** **E** **↵** to extract records

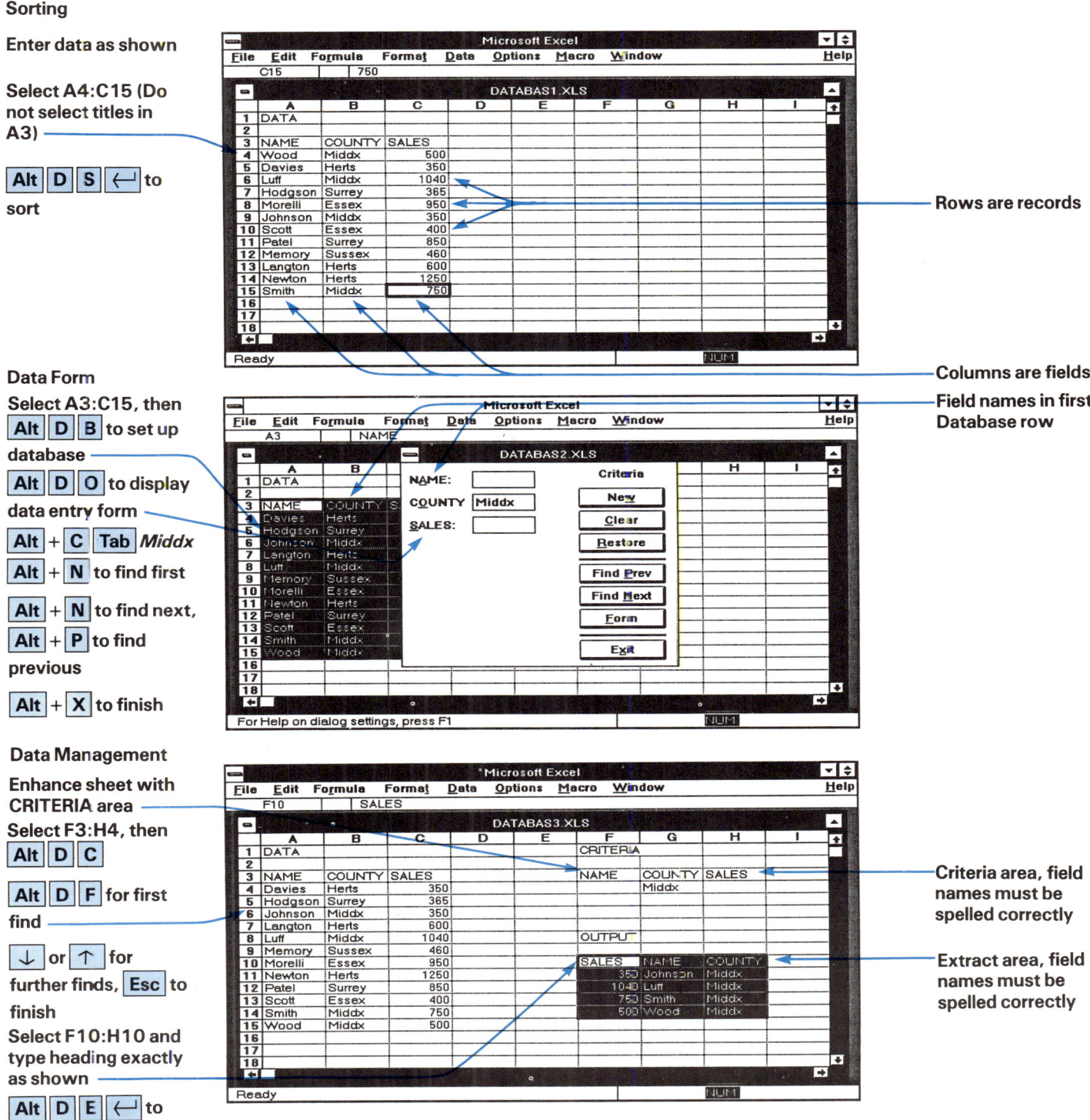

Rows are records

Columns are fields

Field names in first Database row

Criteria area, field names must be spelled correctly

Extract area, field names must be spelled correctly

Multiple Sheets

Excel lets you combine information from different worksheets. This makes it easy to break your work into several small sheets that are easier to work with than one large one.

Instructions

- Open *trade3* or a similar worksheet. (Choose **Options, Unprotect Document** if required.)
- Type over A1 with the title *Region 1* and re-save the sheet under the new name *region1*.
- Build Region 2's sheet based on Region 1's. Select the range A1:F8 on *region1* and choose **Edit, Copy** to start a copy operation. Choose **File, New** and press **Enter** to accept the **Worksheet** option. The new sheet displays on top of *region1*. Select cell A1 on the new sheet and choose **Edit, Paste** to complete the copy operation.
- Change the title in A1 to *Region 2*, select B4:D5, enter revenue and cost figures like those in the illustration and save the new sheet as *region2*.
- Create a new sheet for the consolidation of both regions for quarter 1. Choose **File, New** and press **Enter**. Fill in the title *Quarter 1 Consolidation* in A1. Type in the labels as shown in the illustration with a column for each region's first quarter totals.
- Choose **Window, Arrange All** to view all three sheets side by side.
- Click the mouse on the *region1* sheet or press **Ctrl+F6** to move there. Then, select E4:E6 and choose **Edit, Copy** to start a copy operation. Move back to the consolidation sheet with the mouse or **Ctrl+F6**. Select cell B4 and choose **Edit, Paste Link**.
- Use the same procedure to link E4:E6 of *region2* to column C of the consolidated sheet.
- Set up a totalling formula in column D of the consolidated sheet. Enter the formula $=sum(b4:c4)$ in D4, select D4:D6 and choose **Edit, Fill Down** to replicate the formula.
- Save the consolidated sheet under a name like *consol1*. Then save the whole workspace using **File, Save Workspace**. You can call the workspace *consol1*, too.
- Try changing a figure such as *Jan Revenue* on the *region2* sheet. Notice the change to *consol1*.

Helpful tips

To refer to a cell in another sheet, precede the cell address with the name of the sheet followed by an exclamation point, for example, *REGION1.XLS!$D$4:$D$6*. References to cells in another sheet are usually 'absolute' which means the column and row are preceded by a dollar sign and they do not adjust when the data is moved.

The illustration shows a 'hot link' between sheets. The *consol1* worksheet is a *dependent* sheet. *Region1* and *region2* are *supporting* documents. Changes to the supporting sheets are automatically updated in the dependent sheet. When the links between documents are simple references, you do not need the supporting documents open while working on the dependent document. If the links involve a calculation or function, the supporting documents must be opened, too.

The file name in an external reference to a closed sheet on disk must be surrounded by apostrophes, for example, *'REGION1.XLS'!$D$4:$D$6*.

The formula for a link is an *array* formula which means that it is surrounded by braces, { and }, and that the one formula applies to a range of cells. In the example, Excel handled this automatically. Note that you cannot edit individual cells in an array range like B4:B6 in the *consol1* sheet.

Instead of a live link, you can also use **Edit, Paste Special** to 'consolidate' figures. **Paste Special** lets you add to, rather than overwrite, the cells you're pasting into. It also allows you to subtract, multiply or divide.

Multiple Sheets

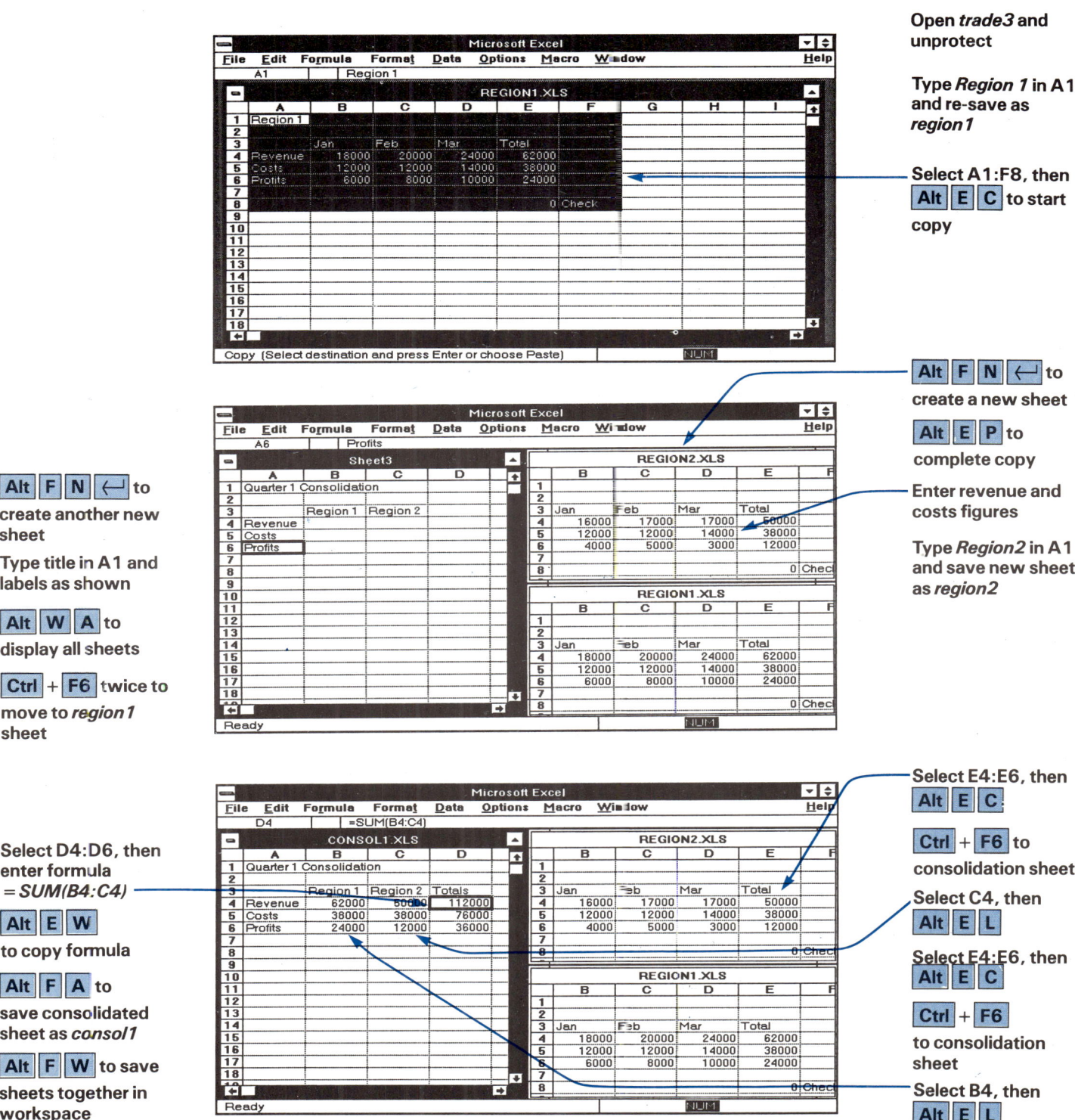

Open *trade3* and unprotect

Type *Region 1* in A1 and re-save as *region1*

Select A1:F8, then `Alt` `E` `C` to start copy

`Alt` `F` `N` `⏎` to create a new sheet

`Alt` `E` `P` to complete copy

Enter revenue and costs figures

Type *Region2* in A1 and save new sheet as *region2*

`Alt` `F` `N` `⏎` to create another new sheet

Type title in A1 and labels as shown

`Alt` `W` `A` to display all sheets

`Ctrl` + `F6` twice to move to *region1* sheet

Select E4:E6, then `Alt` `E` `C`

`Ctrl` + `F6` to consolidation sheet

Select C4, then `Alt` `E` `L`

Select E4:E6, then `Alt` `E` `C`

`Ctrl` + `F6` to consolidation sheet

Select B4, then `Alt` `E` `L`

Select D4:D6, then enter formula = *SUM(B4:C4)*

`Alt` `E` `W` to copy formula

`Alt` `F` `A` to save consolidated sheet as *consol1*

`Alt` `F` `W` to save sheets together in workspace

Enhancing Printouts

This example shows how to improve the appearance of a printed worksheet using headers, footers and fonts. It also illustrates how to print out only part of a sheet.

Instructions

- Open a worksheet such as *cash1*.
- Delete the title from A1.
- Choose **File, Page Setup**. In **Header**, fill in the left, centre and right pieces of the header. Type *&LIllustrium Ltd&CQ1&&Q2 Cash Forecast&R&D*. (See the tips below for an explanation of the & codes.) Switch off **Row & Column Headings** and **Gridlines**. Press **Enter**.
- Choose **File, Print**, and press **Enter**.
- To print just quarter 2, select E1:G18 and choose **Options, Set Print Area**.
- Select column A and change to an italic font using **Format, Font**.
- With column A still selected, choose **Options, Set Print Titles**.
- Choose **File, Page Setup**. Remove *Q1&&* from the **Header** and press **Enter**.
- Choose **File, Print** switch on **Preview** and press **Enter**. Excel shows you a miniature of the printed report.
- Position the magnifying glass over a part of the report and press **Z** to **Zoom** in on a part of the report. Press **P** to **Print** the report.
- Re-save the worksheet to keep the **Page Setup** settings.

Helpful tips

You can print sideways if your printer supports landscape printing. To switch to landscape printing, choose **File, Printer Setup, Setup** and switch on the **Landscape** option if shown.

Headers and **Footers** in **File, Page Setup** can contain special control codes for formatting:

Code	Meaning	Code	Meaning
&L	Align to left	&D	Insert date
&R	Align to right	&T	Insert time
&C	Centre	&F	Insert file name
&B	Print bold	&P	Insert page number
&I	Print italic	&P+n or &P−n	Adjust the page number by n
&&	Print an ampersand		

Headers and footers automatically print .5 inch from the edge of the paper.

Since Excel is WYSIWYG, the fonts you see on screen are the fonts which print. To make full use of your printer's fonts, apply fonts to the worksheet using the **Format, Font** menu. Four fonts are allowed per worksheet.

If you want to change the four fonts available, choose **Format, Font**, pick one of the four option buttons, then choose **Fonts**. On the dialogue box, switch on **Printer Fonts**. Select the font and point size that you would like to appear on the **Format, Font** menu, and press **OK** or **Replace**. This places the new font on the menu and changes the font of the current selection on the worksheet.

Press **Ctrl+** a number **1** to **4** to style the selected cells in the corresponding font from the **Format, Font** menu.

To reset the Print Area or Print Titles, select a new area and choose **Options, Set Print Area** or **Set Print Titles**. To remove the title and/or print area definitions completely, choose **Formula, Define Name** and delete the names **Print_Titles** and/or **Print_Area**.

Enhancing Printouts

Open *cash 1*

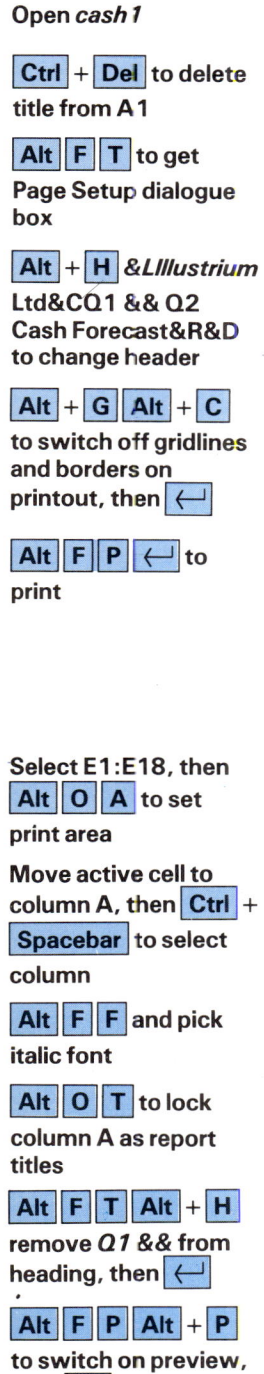

Ctrl + **Del** to delete title from A1

Alt **F** **T** to get Page Setup dialogue box

Alt + **H** *&LIllustrium* **Ltd&CQ1 && Q2 Cash Forecast&R&D** to change header

Alt + **G** **Alt** + **C** to switch off gridlines and borders on printout, then ↵

Alt **F** **P** ↵ to print

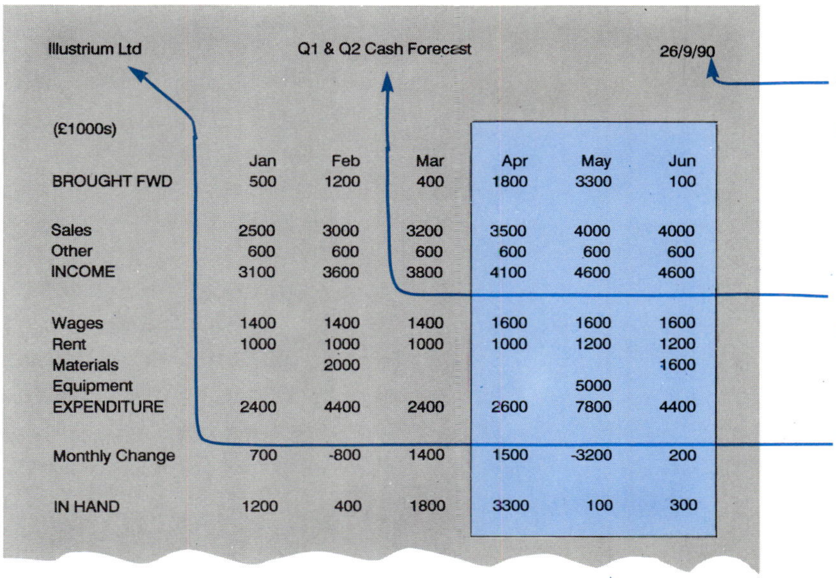

Select E1:E18, then **Alt** **O** **A** to set print area

Move active cell to column A, then **Ctrl** + **Spacebar** to select column

Alt **F** **F** and pick italic font

Alt **O** **T** to lock column A as report titles

Alt **F** **T** **Alt** + **H** remove *Q1 &&* from heading, then ↵

Alt **F** **P** **Alt** + **P** to switch on preview, then ↵

P to print

Re-save sheet to keep print settings

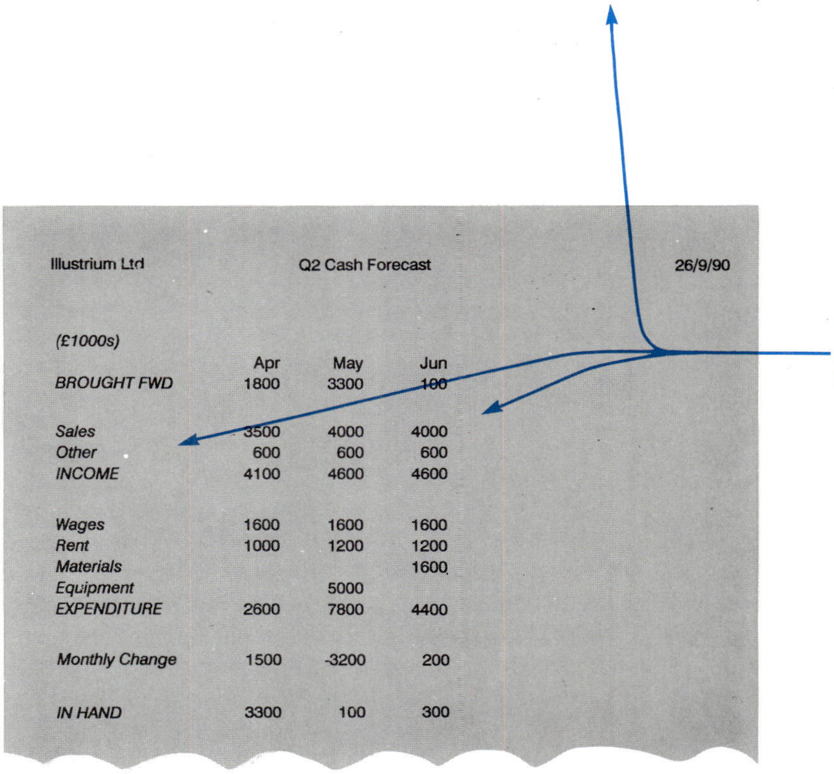

Illustrium Ltd		Q1 & Q2 Cash Forecast			26/9/90	
(£1000s)	Jan	Feb	Mar	Apr	May	Jun
BROUGHT FWD	500	1200	400	1800	3300	100
Sales	2500	3000	3200	3500	4000	4000
Other	600	600	600	600	600	600
INCOME	3100	3600	3800	4100	4600	4600
Wages	1400	1400	1400	1600	1600	1600
Rent	1000	1000	1000	1000	1200	1200
Materials		2000				1600
Equipment					5000	
EXPENDITURE	2400	4400	2400	2600	7800	4400
Monthly Change	700	-800	1400	1500	-3200	200
IN HAND	1200	400	1800	3300	100	300

&R is right aligned

&D is date

&C is centred

&L is left aligned

Illustrium Ltd		Q2 Cash Forecast		26/9/90
(£1000s)	Apr	May	Jun	
BROUGHT FWD	1800	3300	100	
Sales	3500	4000	4000	
Other	600	600	600	
INCOME	4100	4600	4600	
Wages	1600	1600	1600	
Rent	1000	1200	1200	
Materials			1600	
Equipment		5000		
EXPENDITURE	2600	7800	4400	
Monthly Change	1500	-3200	200	
IN HAND	3300	100	300	

Only data in Print Area and Print Titles is printed

Enhancing Graphs

Excel gives you a wide variety of techniques for developing charts quickly and polishing them up into 'presentation' quality graphics.

Instructions

- Create a new sheet like the one shown in the illustration and save it.
- Select A4:G7 and press **F11**, the shortcut to creating a new chart.
- Maximise the chart window by clicking on the maximise button with the mouse or pressing **Ctrl+F10**.
- Choose **Gallery, Line**, select the first style of line chart and press **Enter**.
- Choose **Chart, Add Legend**.
- Give the chart a title by choosing **Chart, Attach Text, Chart Title**. The word 'Title' appears surrounded by small square 'handles' which show that it is currently selected.
- Press **F2** to edit the default 'Title'. Type in **Cost Analysis**, press **Ctrl+Enter** to start a new line, type *Quarters 1 and 2*, and press **Enter**.
- With the title still selected, choose **Format, Patterns**, or double-click on the title with the mouse. At the top of the dialogue box, pick **Automatic**, switch on **Shadow** and press the **Font** command button. Switch on **Bold** and **Italic**, then press **Enter** or click on **OK**.
- To place a description beside the Y-axis, choose **Chart, Attach Text**, pick **Value Axis**, and press **Enter**. The letter 'Y' appears surrounded by handles.
- Press **F2** to edit the label. Type in *Costs* and press **Enter**.
- Double-click on Costs and press the **Text** button or choose **Format, Text**. Switch on **Vertical Text**. Press the **Font** button, switch on **Bold** and press **Enter**.
- Place an arrow by choosing **Chart, Add Arrow**. Using the mouse, shorten the arrow by pointing to one of the black handles at the end of the arrow and dragging. (If the arrow moves instead of shortens, release the mouse button and point more accurately at the handle.) Move the arrow into place by pointing to the body of the arrow, instead of its handles, and dragging. Rotate the arrow by pointing to one of the arrow's handles and dragging. If the handles disappear, simply click on the arrow.
- Place a note at the end of the arrow. Click somewhere on the neutral backgrouund of the chart or choose **Chart, Select Chart**. Press **F2**, type in *Note: Seasonal*, press **Ctrl+Enter**, type *Fluctuation* and press **Enter**. The note appears, surrounded by handles. (It will probably overlap another part of the chart.)
- Point to the note and drag it to the end of the arrow. Then, double-click on the note, and choose **Font**, or with the keyboard choose **Format, Font**. Select a smaller point size and click on **OK** or press **Enter**.
- Click on the neutral background to remove all handles and view the chart clearly.
- Save and print the chart in the usual way.

Helpful tips

A chart is composed of many objects. Click on the various lines and symbols and watch where the handles appear. Nearly every object can be separately styled by double-clicking on it.

The **Automatic** or **Invisible** option on most format dialogue boxes restores an object to its original appearance.

Enhancing Graphs

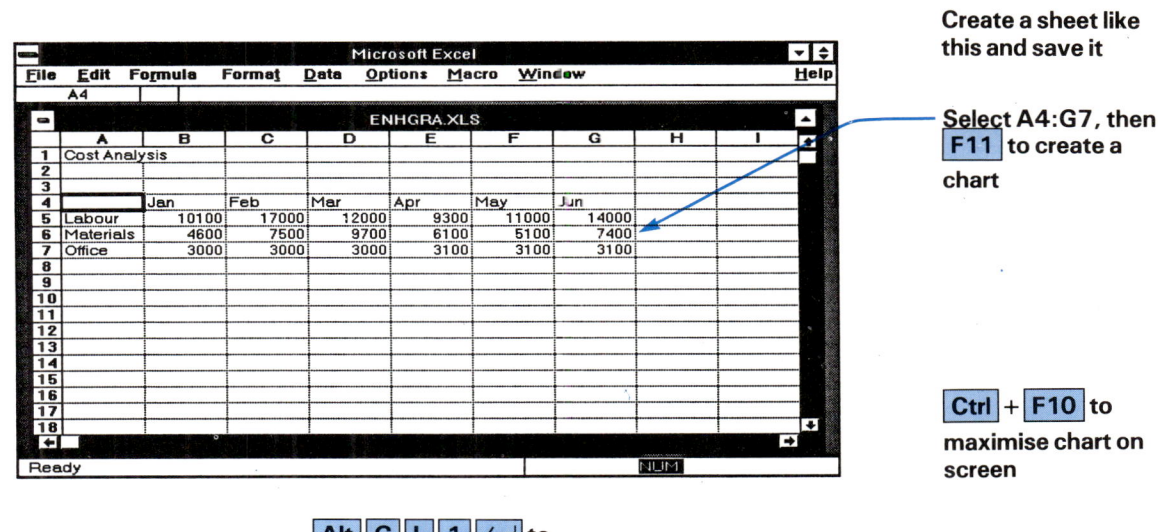

Create a sheet like this and save it

Select A4:G7, then `F11` **to create a chart**

The spreadsheet shows:

	A	B	C	D	E	F	G	H	I
1	Cost Analysis								
2									
3									
4		Jan	Feb	Mar	Apr	May	Jun		
5	Labour	10100	17000	12000	9300	11000	14000		
6	Materials	4600	7500	9700	6100	5100	7400		
7	Office	3000	3000	3000	3100	3100	3100		

`Ctrl` + `F10` **to maximise chart on screen**

`Alt` `G` `L` `1` `⏎` **to switch to a line chart**

`Alt` `C` `T` `Alt` + `T` **to make title appear**

`F2` **backspace over 'Title', type** *Cost Analysis* `Ctrl` + `⏎` *Quarters 1 and 2* `⏎`

`Alt` `T` `P` `Alt` + `A` `Alt` + `H` `Alt` + `O` `Alt` + `B` `Alt` + `I` `⏎` **to format title as shown**

`Alt` `C` `T` `Alt` + `V` `⏎` **to attach a Y-axis label**

`F2` **backspace over 'Y', type** *Costs* `⏎`

`Alt` `T` `T` `Alt` + `V` `Alt` + `O` `Alt` + `B` `⏎` **to format label as shown**

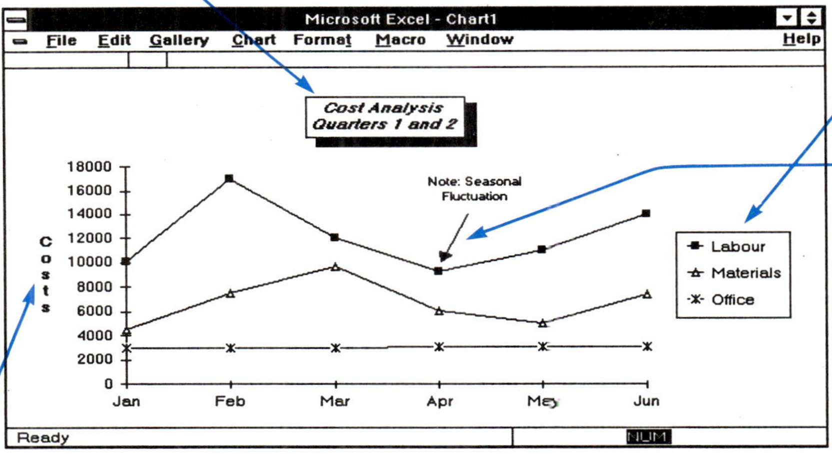

`Alt` `C` `L` **to add legend**

`Alt` `C` `R` **to place arrow**

Size and move with mouse by dragging

Click on background, then `F2` *Note: Seasonal* `Ctrl` + `⏎` *Fluctuation* `⏎`

Drag note into position with mouse

`Alt` `T` `F` **choose smaller point size, then** `⏎`

Functions and Names

This example introduces some of the more common Excel functions and illustrates the use of names as a device for making worksheet formulas more understandable.

Instructions

- Open the *cash1* worksheet.
- Select the range B6:G6. Choose **Formula, Define Names**. Excel has guessed that you want to use the label in A6, *Sales*, as the name for the selected range. Press **Enter**.
- Repeat the process for *Equipment* in B13:G13 and *In Hand* in B18:G18. Notice that Excel substitutes an underscore for a space giving *In__Hand*.
- Enter the labels in column A under *MESSAGES* and *ANALYSIS*.
- Enter the labels in columns A through C under *MESSAGE STORAGE*.
- In cell B22, choose **Formula, Paste Function**, press the letter *I* to move the highlight to the **IF** function, and press **Enter**. Excel transfers the function to the formula bar and the insertion point is positioned between parentheses. Type *B16⟨0,A32* and press **F4**. This converts the relative reference A32 into the absolute reference $A$32. Continue by typing a comma, then *B32*, and press **F4** again. The whole formula should read *=IF(B16⟨0,$A$32,$B$32)*. Press **Enter**.
- Using the same techniques, in B23 enter the formula *=IF(B18⟨500,IF(B18⟨250,$C$33,$A$33),$B$33)*.
- Use **Edit, Copy** or **Edit, Fill Right** to copy B22:B23 to C22:G23. Notice that the absolute references, with dollar signs, don't adjust.
- Enter the statistical functions as shown on the illustration in cells B26:B29.

Helpful tips

Naming ranges has many advantages. Range names are usually easier to remember, quicker to write and easier to understand in formulas than cell references. Avoid range names that might be misinterpreted as cell references. For example, AC102 might look like a good name for Account 102, but it could be mistaken by Excel for Column AC, row 102.

Absolute references don't get adjusted automatically when you move or copy cells. Pressing **F4** while writing or editing a formula makes a cell reference absolute. If you forget to press **F4** while entering a formula, you can edit the cell later. Press **F2**, position the insertion point at the reference and press **F4**.

In some cases you may want either the column or the row address to be absolute, but not both. Press **F4** repeatedly to change parts of the address from absolute to relative.

The **IF** function is a decision-making function with three parts. The first parameter is a test for a condition such as whether two values are equal. The second part tells what to do if the condition is true and the third parameter tells what to do when the test is false. The parameters are separated by a comma.

The **IF** function can perform six texts: =Equal to, ⟨Less than, ⟩Greater than, ⟨=Less than or equal to, ⟩=Greater than or equal to, ⟨⟩Unequal to. You can combine conditions by nesting them inside **AND, OR** and **NOT** functions.

Functions can be 'nested' which means that you can use a function as a parameter inside the parentheses of another function. Pay careful attention to commas and matching pairs of left and right parentheses.

Switch on **Paste Arguments** when using **Formula, Paste Function** to have Excel prompt you with a reminder of the parameters needed. Press **F2** to edit and replace the prompts with genuine parameters.

Functions and Names

Open *cash1* or similar

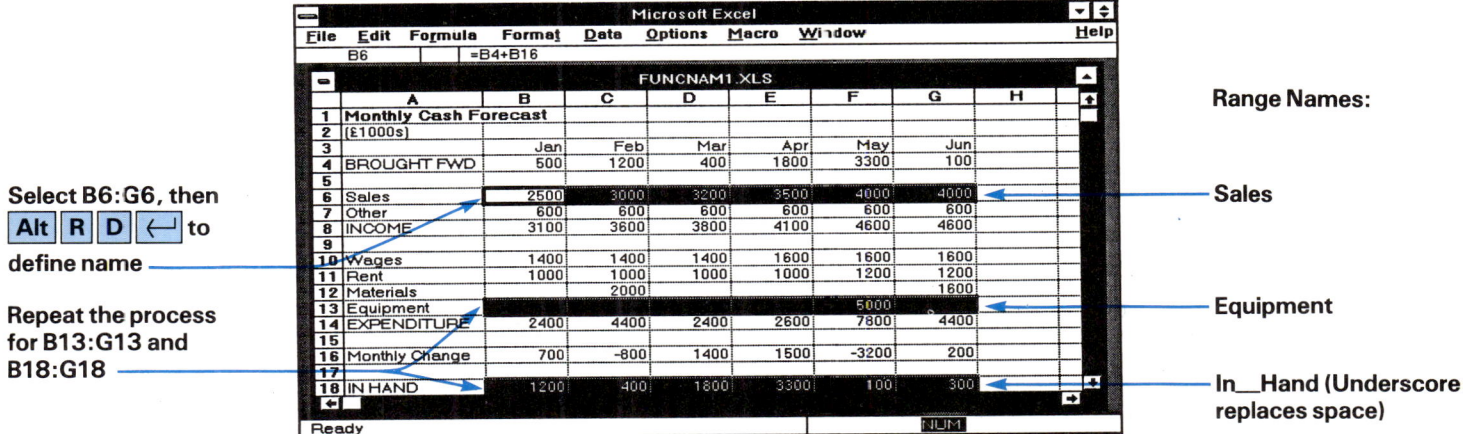

Select B6:G6, then
Alt R D ⏎ to
define name

Repeat the process
for B13:G13 and
B18:G18

Range Names:

Sales

Equipment

In__Hand (Underscore
replaces space)

Enter labels in
column A and rows
32 and 33

Alt R T / ⏎ to
paste IF function in
B22 and B23

Type in formulas
shown at bottom of
illustration

Enter formulas

= *MAX(Sales)*

= *MIN(Sales)*

= *AVERAGE*
(In__hand)

= *COUNT*
(Equipment)

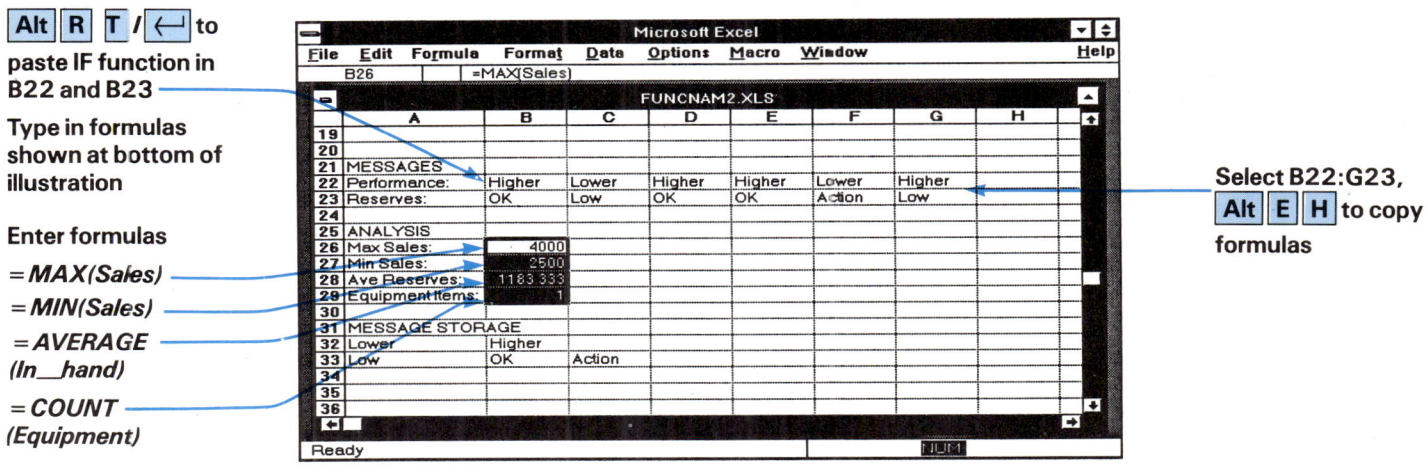

Select B22:G23,
Alt E H to copy
formulas

Formulas:

B22 = IF(B16⟨0,$A$32,$B$32)
B23 = IF(B18⟨500,IF(B18⟨250,$C$33,$A$33),$B$33)
All functions must have matching open and closed parentheses
F4 to convert to absolute cell references

Conversion Table

A variety of worksheet techniques are combined in this exercise to produce an Imperial to Metric conversion table.

Instructions

- Start a new worksheet.
- Type in the label Conversion *Table1* in A1.
- Select A3:E3, widen the columns to 15 and type in the labels shown in the illustration. With row 3 still selected, choose **Format, Border** and switch on **Top** and **Bottom** borders.
- Select B5:B17, type in the labels in column B, then choose **Format, Alignment, Right**.
- Type in the labels in column E.
- Type in the conversion factors in column C.
- Enter the formula shown in D5. You can type in the whole formula manually but here's how to use a technique called pointing: Choose **Formula, Paste Function**, press the letter *I* to select the **IF** function and press **Enter**. Use the arrow key to point to A5, or click on A5 with the mouse. A flashing border surrounds A5 and *A5* appears in the formular bar. Continue typing the next part of the formula =*0,NA*, then point to A5, type * which means multiply, point to C5, and press **Enter**.
- Select D5:D17 and choose **Edit, Fill Down** to copy the formula to the rest of the column.
- Make a cell in column C the active cell, choose **Format, Column Widlth**, set a new width of zero, and press **Enter**.
- Select A5:A17, choose **Edit, Cell Protection**, switch off **Locked** and press **Enter**.
- Protect the worksheet using **Options, Protect Document**.
- Try out the sheet by entering values in column A.
- Save the sheet for future reference.

Helpful tips

Pointing is a useful technique for filling cell and range addresses in formulas. While typing in a formula, use the arrow keys or mouse to point to a cell. The cell address that appears automatically in the formula changes as you move the arrow key or mouse. To stop pointing, just resume typing.

To enter a range using pointing, point to the start of the range. Using the keyboard, hold the **Shift** key and point to the end of the range. Using the mouse, drag to the end of the range.

If you are in Edit mode (you have pressed **F2** to edit an existing formula), press **F2** a second time to enable cell pointing.

The **NA** function lets your formula signal know that there is insufficient information to return a meaningful value, instead of displaying blank or zero which might sometimes be a valid result.

If you make a mistake while entering a formula, Excel displays a message and automatically switches into **Edit** mode. You must either correct the error or press **Esc** in order to leave the cell. If you press **Esc**, you will lose your partially completed formula which is sometimes very inconvenient. To avoid this problem, press **Home** to position to the beginning of the formula, insert a space, and press **Enter** to temporarily store the formula as a label while you investigate the problem.

As well as hiding a column by reducing its width to zero, you can also hide formulas. Select the range of cells with formulas to hide. Choose **Format, Cell Protection**, switch on **Hidden**, then choose **Options, Protect Document**. The values of hidden cells remain visible, but the formula does not appear in the formula bar.

Conversion Table

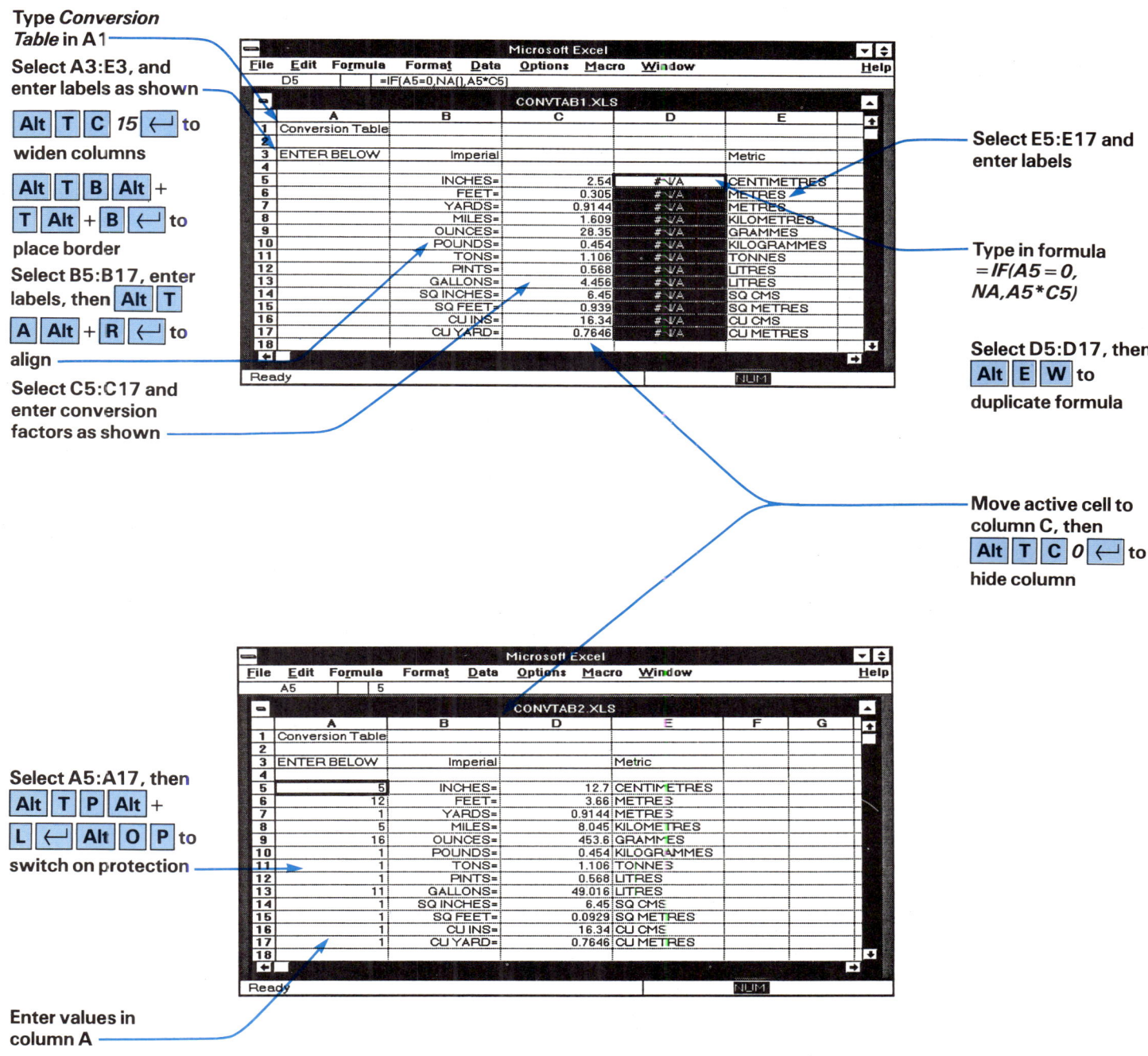

Type *Conversion Table* in A1

Select A3:E3, and enter labels as shown

Alt T C 15 ← to widen columns

Alt T B Alt +
T Alt + B ← to place border

Select B5:B17, enter labels, then Alt T
A Alt + R ← to align

Select C5:C17 and enter conversion factors as shown

Select E5:E17 and enter labels

Type in formula =IF(A5=0, NA,A5*C5)

Select D5:D17, then Alt E W to duplicate formula

Move active cell to column C, then Alt T C 0 ← to hide column

Select A5:A17, then Alt T P Alt +
L ← Alt O P to switch on protection

Enter values in column A

First screenshot (CONVTAB1.XLS):

D5 =IF(A5=0,NA(),A5*C5)

	A	B	C	D	E
1	Conversion Table				
2					
3	ENTER BELOW	Imperial			Metric
4					
5		INCHES=	2.54	#N/A	CENTIMETRES
6		FEET=	0.305	#N/A	METRES
7		YARDS=	0.9144	#N/A	METRES
8		MILES=	1.609	#N/A	KILOMETRES
9		OUNCES=	28.35	#N/A	GRAMMES
10		POUNDS=	0.454	#N/A	KILOGRAMMES
11		TONS=	1.106	#N/A	TONNES
12		PINTS=	0.568	#N/A	LITRES
13		GALLONS=	4.456	#N/A	LITRES
14		SQ INCHES=	6.45	#N/A	SQ CMS
15		SQ FEET=	0.939	#N/A	SQ METRES
16		CU INS=	16.34	#N/A	CU CMS
17		CU YARD=	0.7646	#N/A	CU METRES
18					

Second screenshot (CONVTAB2.XLS):

A5 5

	A	B	D	E	F	G
1	Conversion Table					
2						
3	ENTER BELOW	Imperial		Metric		
4						
5	5	INCHES=	12.7	CENTIMETRES		
6	12	FEET=	3.66	METRES		
7	1	YARDS=	0.9144	METRES		
8	5	MILES=	8.045	KILOMETRES		
9	16	OUNCES=	453.6	GRAMMES		
10	1	POUNDS=	0.454	KILOGRAMMES		
11	1	TONS=	1.106	TONNES		
12	1	PINTS=	0.568	LITRES		
13	11	GALLONS=	49.016	LITRES		
14	1	SQ INCHES=	6.45	SQ CMS		
15	1	SQ FEET=	0.0929	SQ METRES		
16	1	CU INS=	16.34	CU CMS		
17	1	CU YARD=	0.7646	CU METRES		
18						

Investments

This example uses Excel in a typical financial application. Net Present Value is useful for comparing investments with different cash returns over the same period.

Instructions

- Type in the labels in column A.
- Then using the mouse, position the mouse pointer in the worksheet border between columns A and B until the mouse pointer changes to a double-headed arrow, and drag to widen column A.
- Type in the labels in row 5. Widen columns B, C and D with the mouse. Select all three columns by dragging over the column letters, position the mouse pointer on the worksheet border between any two of the columns until the mouse pointer changes, then drag to widen all three columns at once.
- Type in an interest (also called 'discount') rate in B3.
- Type in the sums invested in row 7.
- Enter the cash returns expected in each of the three years in rows 9 through 11.
- Calculate the undiscounted cash flow in B13 with the formula *=sum(b9:b11)*.
- The NPV function needs two pieces of information: the interest rate and the cash flows. In this example, we are comparing all three investments assuming the same interest rate. The formula is *=NPV($B$3,B9:B11)*. Choose **Formula, Paste Function**, press *N* until the **NPV** function is selected, then press **Enter**. Point to cell B3 to fill in the rate, and press **F4** to turn it into an absolute address. Type in comma, then point to the range B9:B11 to identify the cash flows. Press **Enter**.
- Compute the profitability by subtracting the original investment from the result of the Excel **NPV** function. In cell B16, enter the formula *=B14-B7*.
- Select the range B13:D16 and choose **Edit, Fill Right** to finish the calculations for the remaining columns.
- The pennies are meaningless to sums like these and they clutter the display. Use the **ROUND** function to remove the decimal places from the NPV calculation. Press **F2** to edit the formula in B14 to *=ROUND(NPV($B$3,B9:B11),0)*.
- Copy the improved formula to C14:D14.

Helpful tips

NPV is just one of the dozen powerful financial functions available in Excel. See the *Excel Reference* at the back of the book for a list of some of the others.

An accountant's interpretation of Net Present Value usually requires that you subtract the amount of the original investment from the result obtained from the Excel **NPV** function.

Entering a number followed by a percent sign automatically formats the cell as a percentage. If you change the value of a percentage cell, be sure to enter the new value with a percent sign or as a decimal.

If you forget to press **F4** while entering a formula to convert to an absolute reference, you can edit the cell later using **F2**, position to the address and press **F4**.

Assign a name for the discount rate in B3 to make your formulas more readable.

For removing unwanted decimal places, using the **ROUND** function is usually preferable to changing the cell format.

Investments

Type labels in column A

Type in discount rate as a percent

Select B7:D7 and enter amounts invested

Type in annual return

Enter formula = *SUM(B9:B11)*

Alt R T to paste NPV function, then edit to = *NPV($B$3, B9:B11)*

Enter formula = *B14-B7*

Position mouse pointer in the border between columns then drag to widen

Widen columns B, C and D

Enter labels

Select B13:D16, then Alt E H to copy formulas

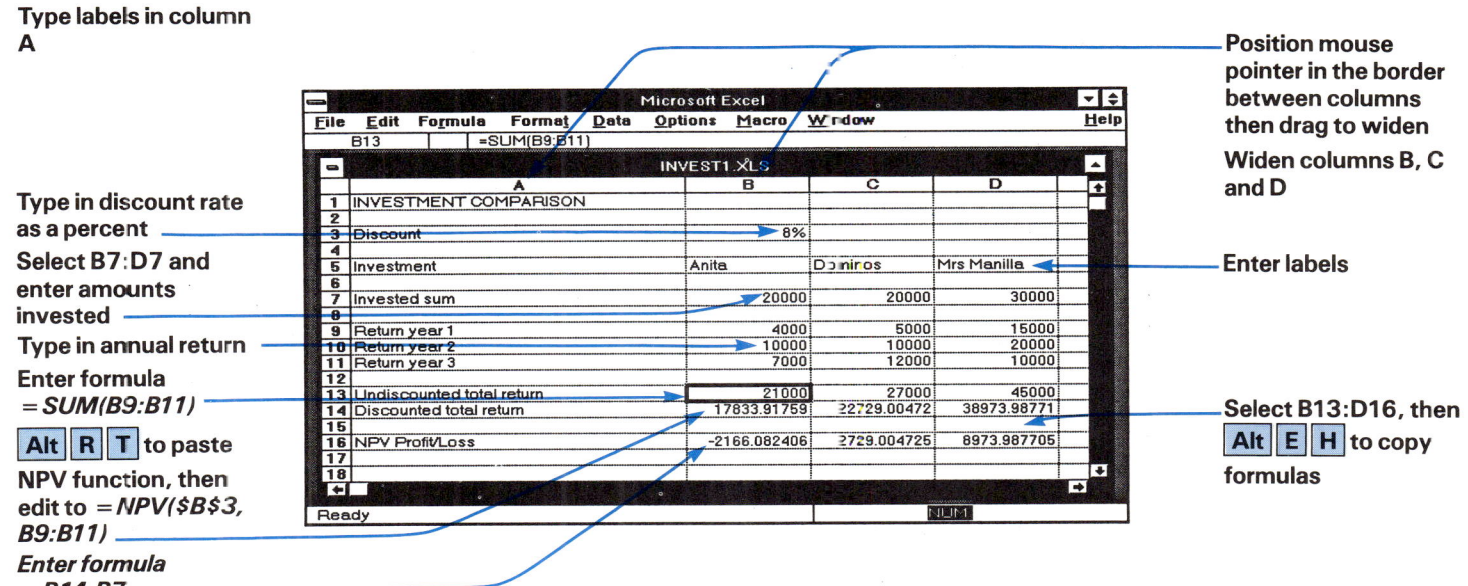

B13   =SUM(B9:B11)

INVEST1.XLS

	A	B	C	D
1	INVESTMENT COMPARISON			
2				
3	Discount	8%		
4				
5	Investment	Anita	Dominos	Mrs Manilla
6				
7	Invested sum	20000	20000	30000
8				
9	Return year 1	4000	5000	15000
10	Return year 2	10000	10000	20000
11	Return year 3	7000	12000	10000
12				
13	Undiscounted total return	21000	27000	45000
14	Discounted total return	17833.91759	22729.00472	38973.98771
15				
16	NPV Profit/Loss	-2166.082406	2729.004725	8973.987705
17				
18				

Ready   NUM

F2 , then edit to = *ROUND(NPV ($B$3,B9:B11),0)* to remove decimal places

Unlock data entry areas and protect worksheet

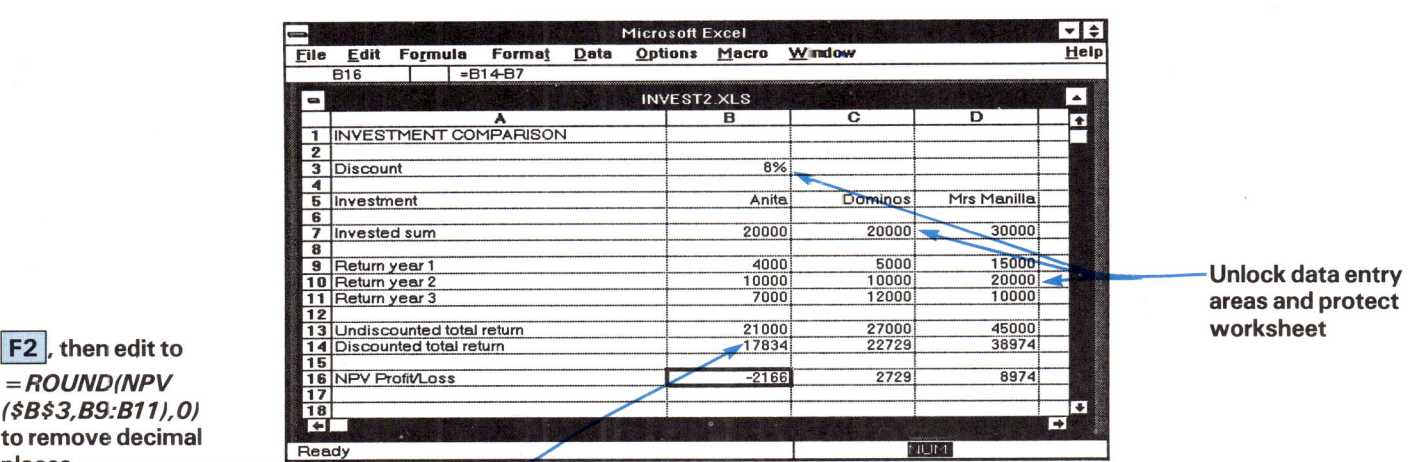

B16   =B14-B7

INVEST2.XLS

	A	B	C	D
1	INVESTMENT COMPARISON			
2				
3	Discount	8%		
4				
5	Investment	Anita	Dominos	Mrs Manilla
6				
7	Invested sum	20000	20000	30000
8				
9	Return year 1	4000	5000	15000
10	Return year 2	10000	10000	20000
11	Return year 3	7000	12000	10000
12				
13	Undiscounted total return	21000	27000	45000
14	Discounted total return	17834	22729	38974
15				
16	NPV Profit/Loss	-2166	2729	8974
17				
18				

Ready   NUM

Macros

A macro is a set of instructions for automating a task. Excel has two types of macros. A *Command Macro* works like a robot at the keyboard. When you start a command macro, it drives Excel as though you were typing in each command yourself. A *Function Macro* is a custom set of calculations that work like Excel's built-in functions. This example shows you how to use Excel's macro recording feature to create a command macro for simplifying repetitive tasks.

Instructions

A label (text) is usually aligned left in a cell, but often it looks better to align labels over a column of numbers to the right. Here's how to create a macro to do this and use it as a keyboard shortcut.

- Open a worksheet like *trade1* or a create a new one.
- Select a cell with a label aligned left over a column of numbers.
- Begin 'recording' a command macro. Choose **Macro, Record**, type in a name like *alignright*, **Tab**, type in the letter *r* as the keyboard shortcut, and press **Enter**. Notice the word 'Recording' in the status bar at the bottom of the screen.
- Execute the sequence of instructions you want to record. In this case, it is **Format, Alignment, Right, Enter**.
- End the recording session by choosing **Macro, Stop Recording**.
- Try out the new macro. Select another cell to format and press **Ctrl+R**.

Here's how to create a macro to double-underline final totals.

- Position the active cell in an empty row.
- Choose **Macro, Record**, type in the name *doubleunderline*, press **Tab**, type in the letter *u*, and press **Enter**.
- Execute this sequence of instructions to create a double underline. Choose **Format, Row Height**, type in *2*, and press **Enter**. Choose **Format, Border**, switch on **Top** and **Bottom**, and press **Enter**.
- Choose **Macro, Stop Recording**.
- Select several cells in the same or another empty row, and press **Ctrl+U** to try out the macro.

Behind the scenes, Excel has created a *macro sheet*.

- Press **Ctrl+F6** to move to the macro sheet. (You may need to do this several times if you had a number of worksheets open when you began the example.)
- Move the active cell over cells with formulas and view the cell contents in the formula bar.
- Save the macro sheet like any other worksheet. Choose **File, Save As**, assign a name like *utils*, and press **Enter**.

Helpful tips

If you make a mistake recording a macro, stop recording and start over.

To use a macro sheet in another session later, you must open it first. If you set up macros to use regularly with specific sheets, save a workspace with both the worksheet and macro sheet, then open the workspace.

To open a macro sheet of common utilities each time you start Excel, modify the Windows configuration file, WIN.INI. In the [Microsoft Excel] section of WIN.INI, add the line *OPEN=macrofilename*.

Macros

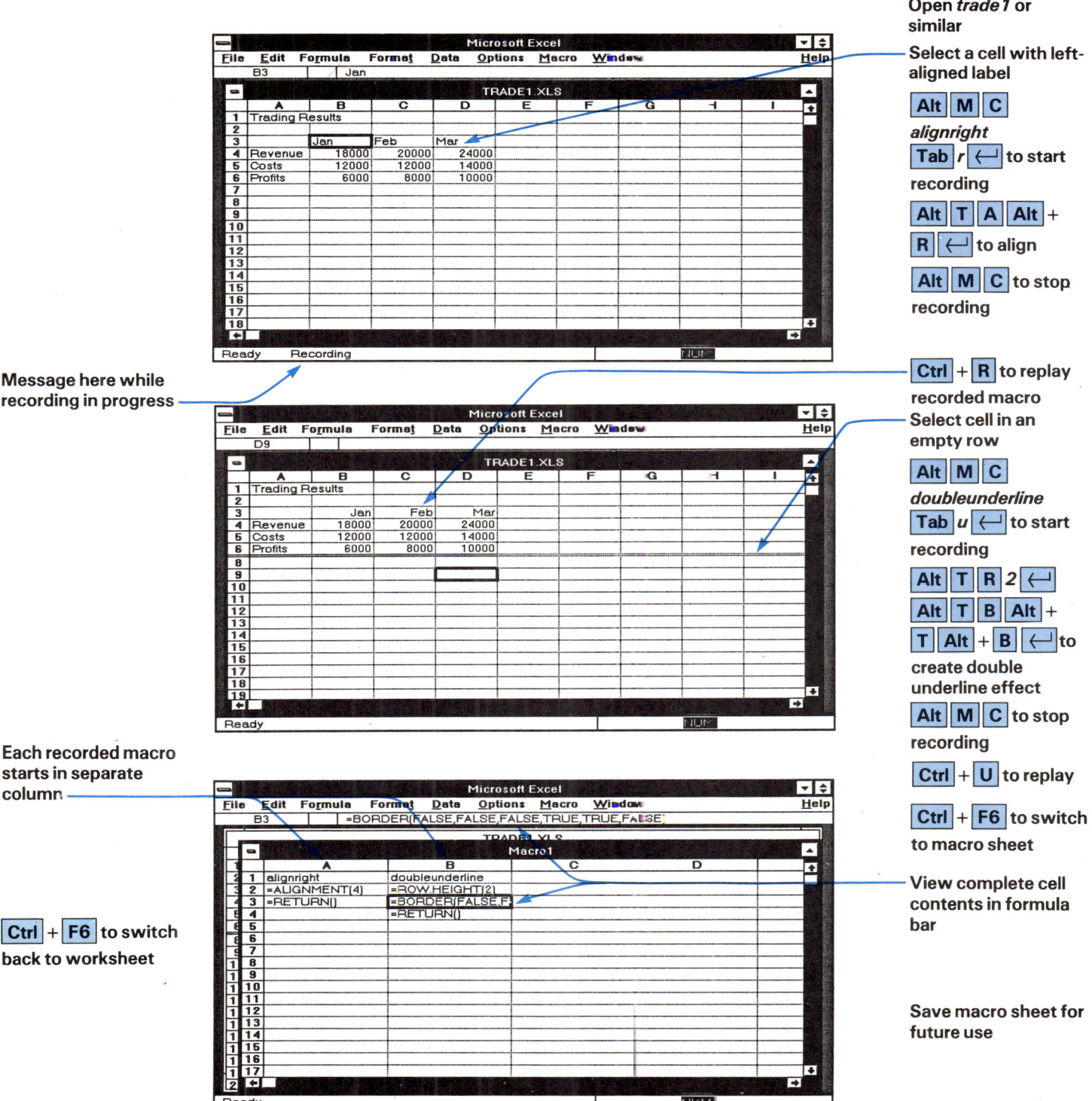

Message here while recording in progress

Each recorded macro starts in separate column

Ctrl + F6 to switch back to worksheet

Open *trade1* or similar

Select a cell with left-aligned label

Alt M C

alignright

Tab *r* ← to start recording

Alt T A Alt + R ← to align

Alt M C to stop recording

Ctrl + R to replay recorded macro

Select cell in an empty row

Alt M C

doubleunderline

Tab *u* ← to start recording

Alt T R *2* ←

Alt T B Alt + T Alt + B ← to create double underline effect

Alt M C to stop recording

Ctrl + U to replay

Ctrl + F6 to switch to macro sheet

View complete cell contents in formula bar

Save macro sheet for future use

Excel Reference

Keys

Function keys

	Key	Shift+Key	Ctrl+Key	Shift+Ctrl+Key
F1	Help	Context-sensitive Help		
F2	Edit Formula	Edit Note	Show Info	
F3	Paste Name	Paste Function	Define Name	Create Name
F4	Absolute/Relative Reference		Close Document Window	
F5	Go to	Formula Find	Restore Document Window	
F6	Next Pane	Previous Pane	Next Document Window	Previous Document Window
F7	Formula Find Next	Formula Find Previous	Move Document Window	
F8	Extend Selection	Add to Selection	Size Document Window	
F9	Calculate All	Calculate Document		
F10	Activate Menu		Maximise Document Window	
F11	New Chart	New Worksheet	New Macro Sheet	
F12	Save As	Save	Open	Print

Worksheet movement keys

Key	Description
↑ ↓ → ←	One cell in direction of the arrow
Home	Column A of this row
End	Rightmost column containing data in this row
Ctrl + Home	Cell A1
Ctrl + End	Bottom rightmost cell with data
Ctrl + →	Skip blocks of adjacent data in this row
Ctrl + ←	
Ctrl + ↑	Skip blocks of adjacent data in this column
Ctrl + ↓	
F5	Go to specific cell address
PageUp	One screenful up or down
PageDown	

Ctrl + PageUp Ctrl + PageDown	One screenful left or right

Using the movement keys with **ScrollLock** turned on moves the window without moving the active cell. Press **Home** with **ScrollLock** on to bring the active cell in the current window.

Worksheet selection keys

Shift + ↑ ↓ → ←	Extend selection one cell in direction of the arrow
Shift + Home	Extend selection to column A of this row
Shift + End	Extend selection to rightmost column containing data in this row
Ctrl + Shift + Home	Extend selection to cell A1
Ctrl + Shift + End	Extend selection to bottom rightmost cell with data
Ctrl + Shift + →	Extend selection over blocks of adjacent data in this row
Ctrl + Shift + ←	
Ctrl + Shift + ↑	Extend selection over blocks of adjacent data in this column
Ctrl + Shift + ↓	
Shift + Spacebar	Select whole row
Ctrl + Spacebar	Select whole column
Ctrl + Shift + Spacebar	Select whole worksheet
Shift + Backspace	Deselect everything but the active cell

Cell editing keys

F2	Change existing cell contents, see Edit mode keys below
Delete	Blank out – with options
Ctrl + Delete	Blank out formula only
Shift + Delete	Cut
Shift + Insert	Paste
Ctrl + Insert	Copy
Ctrl + +	Insert cells
Ctrl + –	Delete cells

Edit mode keys

F2	Begin edit mode
Home	Move to first character on the entry line
End	Move to the last character on the entry line
→ ←	Move one character in the direction of the arrow
Ctrl + →	Move one word in the direction of the arrow
Ctrl + ←	
Backspace	Delete the previous character
Delete	Delete character to the right of the insertion point
Insert	Switch between inserting and overtyping
Esc	Return to the sheet without change
←	Accept the changes and return to the sheet

Control key shortcuts (UK keyboard)

Ctrl + @	General format
Ctrl + !	0.00 format
Ctrl + "	h:mm AM/PM format

43

Ctrl + ?	d-mmmm-yy format
Ctrl + $	Currency format
Ctrl + %	0% format
Ctrl + ^	0.00E+00 format
Ctrl + n	Font n (n=1 to 4)
Ctrl + ?	Select Notes
Ctrl + *	Select current region
Ctrl + /	Select current array
Ctrl + \	Select row differences
Ctrl + |	Select column differences
Ctrl + [	Select direct precedents
Ctrl + {	Select all precedents
Ctrl +]	Select direct dependents
Ctrl + }	Select all dependents
Ctrl + =	Calculate now
Ctrl + ' (apostrophe)	Display formulas toggle

Menu and dialogue box keys

Alt	Select menu bar (Press again to deselect menu bar)
F10	Alternative to select menu bar
/	Alternative to select menu bar (configurable)
Esc	Abandon menu or dialogue box
Ctrl + Break	Abandon menu
→ ←	Move to next item on menu bar
↑ ↓	Move up or down one command on menu
↵	Choose selected command on menu; close dialogue box
Spacebar	On dialogue box: Toggle Checkbox Toggle Option button Press Command Button
Tab	On dialogue box: Move to next item
Alt + *letter*	On dialogue box: Move to item with underline *letter*

Status Bar

Messages

Ready	Excel waiting for data entry or command
Enter	Data being entered into a cell
Point	Pointing being used to supply cell reference in formula
Edit	Editing occurring in formula bar
Find	Data, Find command in progress
Help	Help window active
Copy	Copy and paste operation started
Cut	Cut and paste operation started
Size	Window or chart object being sized
Move	Window or chart object being moved
Split	A window is being split into panes
Recording	Macro recording is in progress

Calculate	Manual calculation selected and worksheet needs recalculation
Circular: *ref*	*ref* is involved in a circular reference

Keyboard indicators

CAPS	CapsLock is on
NUM	NumLock is on
SCRL	ScrollLock is on
OVR	The Insert key has been toggled so that typing overwrites instead of inserting
EXT	F8 has been pressed; the selection extends; alternative to Shift+movement key
ADD	Shift+F8 has been pressed; multiple ranges can be selected
FIX	Fixed Decimals option on; see Options, Workspace

Operators

+	Addition
–	Subtraction
*	Multiplication
/	Division
^	Exponent
=	Equal
>	Greater than
<	Less than
>=	Greater than or equal to
<=	Less than or equal to
<>	Not equal to

Codes

Format Codes

Choosing **Format, Number** displays a dialogue box with a list of Excel's built-in formats. Here is a description of the meaning of the codes in the format. Use these characters to create your own custom formats for entering and displaying data.

0	Always display digit in this position; insert leading/trailing zero, if empty
#	Display digit only if present
.	Decimal point
,	Thousands separator
%	Display as percent (multiplies by 100 for display)
E – E + e – e +	Scientific notation
:$ – +() space	Display actual character; character floats over # positions
\	Displays actual character after \
'text'	Displays *text*
*	Fills rest of column with character after *
@	Text typed into numeric cell appears in place of @
[colour]	Changes cell to *colour*, BLACK, WHITE, RED, GREEN, BLUE, YELLOW, MAGENTA or CYAN
;	Separate format of positive and negative values
d	Day of month no leading zero
dd	Two-digit day of month
ddd	Three letter abbreviation: Mon to Sun
dddd	Day of week spelled out: Monday to Sunday
m	Month, no leading zero

45

mm	Two-digit month
mmm	Three letter abbreviation: Jan to Dec
mmmm	Month spelled out: January to December
yy	Year, no century
yyyy	Century and year
h	Hour, no leading zero
hh	Two-digit hour
m	Minutes, no leading zero
mm	Two-digit minutes
s	Seconds, no leading zero
ss	Two-digit seconds
AM/PM am/pm	12-hour time format
A/P a/p	
− / :	Use as dividers

Header and Footer & Codes

&L	Align to left
&R	Align to right
&C	Centre
&B	Print bold
&I	Print italic
&&	Print an ampersand
&D	Insert date
&T	Insert time
&F	Insert file name
&P	Insert page number
&P+n or &P−n	Adjust the page number by n

Functions

Functions are shortcuts to formulas you might enter yourself. The general format is:
=function(arg1,arg2, . . . argn)

The number of arguments varies with the function and some have no arguments at all. Here is a list of commonly used functions. See the Help screens or manual for the exhaustive list.

Date and Time

=DATE(yy,mm,dd)	Converts yymmdd to a date serial number, the number of days since 1st January 1900
=DATEVALUE(date)	Converts date text to date serial number
=NOW()	Serial number of current date and time (time is a fraction)

Financial

=DDB(cost,salvage,life,period)	200% declining balance depreciation
=FV(rate,nper,pmt,pv,type)	Future value based on periodic constant cash flows
=IRR(estimate,cashflows)	Internal rate of return on an investment
=NPER(rate,pmt,pv,fv,type)	Number of payments of an investment
=NPV(rate,cashflows)	Present value of uneven cash flows
=PMT(rate,nper,pv,fv,type)	Periodic payment of investment
=PV(rate,nper,pmt,fv,type)	Present value of even cash flows
=RATE(nper,pmt,pv,fv,type,estimate)	Rate of return on investment
=SLN(cost,salvage,life)	Straight-line depreciation